MW00681521

Flash™ MX
Motion Graphics

SEOL EUNA

 SYBEX   **YoungJin**.com **Y.**

Acquisitions and Developmental Editor: Mariann Barsolo
Korean Language Editor: Suzie Lee
Translation Editor: Colleen Strand
Production Editor: Kelly Winquist
Book Designer: EO Communication, Sung Woo Yoon
Graphic Illustrator: Seol Euna
Compositor: Danny Hong, Annie Hong, Sarah Lee
Proofreader: Suzie Lee
Cover Designer: Highest
Cover Illustrator: Highest

This English edition published by Sybex Inc.
ⓒ 2002 by YoungJin.com
Originally published in Korea 2002 by YoungJin.com, Seoul, Korea.
All rights reserved.

English edition ⓒ 2002 Sybex Inc. SYBEX Inc., 1151 Marina Village
Parkway, Alameda, CA 94501. World rights reserved. No part of this
publication may be stored in a retrieval system, transmitted, or reproduced
in any way, including but not limited to photocopy, photograph, magnetic,
or other record, without the prior agreement and written permission of the
publisher.

Library of Congress Card Number: 2002106409

ISBN: 0-7821-4125-0

SYBEX and the SYBEX logo are either registered trademarks or
trademarks of SYBEX Inc. in the United States and/or other countries.

TRADEMARKS: YoungJin has attempted throughout this book to
distinguish proprietary trademarks from descriptive terms by following the
capitalization style used by the manufacturer.

The author and publisher have made their best efforts to prepare this book,
and the content is based upon final release software whenever possible.
Portions of the manuscript may be based upon pre-release versions supplied
by software manufacturer(s). The author and the publisher make no
representation or warranties of any kind with regard to the completeness or
accuracy of the contents herein and accept no liability of any kind including
but not limited to performance, merchantability, fitness for any particular
purpose, or any losses or damages of any kind caused or alleged to be
caused directly or indirectly from this book.

Photographs and illustrations used in this book have been downloaded from
publicly accessible file archives and are used in this book for news
reportage purposes only to demonstrate the variety of graphics resources
available via electronic access. Text and images available over the Internet
may be subject to copyright and other rights owned by third parties. Online
availability of text and images does not imply that they may be reused
without the permission of rights holders, although the Copyright Act does
permit certain unauthorized reuse as fair use under 17 U.S.C. Section 107.

Manufactured in Korea

10 9 8 7 6 5 4 3 2 1

Software License Agreement: Terms and Conditions

The media and/or any online materials accompanying this book that are available now or in the future contain programs and/or text files (the "Software") to be used in connection with the book. SYBEX hereby grants to you a license to use the Software, subject to the terms that follow. Your purchase, acceptance, or use of the Software will constitute your acceptance of such terms.

The Software compilation is the property of SYBEX unless otherwise indicated and is protected by copyright to SYBEX or other copyright owner(s) as indicated in the media files (the "Owner(s)"). You are hereby granted a single-user license to use the Software for your personal, noncommercial use only. You may not reproduce, sell, distribute, publish, circulate, or commercially exploit the Software, or any portion thereof, without the written consent of SYBEX and the specific copyright owner(s) of any component software included on this media.

In the event that the Software or components include specific license requirements or end-user agreements, statements of condition, disclaimers, limitations or warranties ("End-User License"), those End-User Licenses supersede the terms and conditions herein as to that particular Software component. Your purchase, acceptance, or use of the Software will constitute your acceptance of such End-User Licenses.

By purchase, use or acceptance of the Software you further agree to comply with all export laws and regulations of the United States as such laws and regulations may exist from time to time.

Software Support

Components of the supplemental Software and any offers associated with them may be supported by the specific Owner(s) of that material, but they are not supported by SYBEX. Information regarding any available support may be obtained from the Owner(s) using the information provided in the appropriate read.me files or listed elsewhere on the media.

Should the manufacturer(s) or other Owner(s) cease to offer support or decline to honor any offer, SYBEX bears no responsibility. This notice concerning support for the Software is provided for your information only. SYBEX is not the agent or principal of the Owner(s), and SYBEX is in no way responsible for providing any support for the Software, nor is it liable or responsible for any support provided, or not provided, by the Owner(s).

Warranty

SYBEX warrants the enclosed media to be free of physical defects for a period of ninety (90) days after purchase. The Software is not available from SYBEX in any other form or media than that enclosed herein or posted to www.sybex.com. If you discover a defect in the media during this warranty period, you may obtain a replacement of identical format at no charge by sending the defective media, postage prepaid, with proof of purchase to:

SYBEX Inc.
Product Support Department
1151 Marina Village Parkway
Alameda, CA 94501
Web: http://www.sybex.com

After the 90-day period, you can obtain replacement media of identical format by sending us the defective disk, proof of purchase, and a check or money order for $10, payable to SYBEX.

Disclaimer

SYBEX makes no warranty or representation, either expressed or implied, with respect to the Software or its contents, quality, performance, merchantability, or fitness for a particular purpose. In no event will SYBEX, its distributors, or dealers be liable to you or any other party for direct, indirect, special, incidental, consequential, or other damages arising out of the use of or inability to use the Software or its contents even if advised of the possibility of such damage. In the event that the Software includes an online update feature, SYBEX further disclaims any obligation to provide this feature for any specific duration other than the initial posting. The exclusion of implied warranties is not permitted by some states. Therefore, the above exclusion may not apply to you. This warranty provides you with specific legal rights; there may be other rights that you may have that vary from state to state. The pricing of the book with the Software by SYBEX reflects the allocation of risk and limitations on liability contained in this agreement of Terms and Conditions.

Shareware Distribution

This Software may contain various programs that are distributed as shareware. Copyright laws apply to both shareware and ordinary commercial software, and the copyright Owner(s) retains all rights. If you try a shareware program and continue using it, you are expected to register it. Individual programs differ on details of trial periods, registration, and payment. Please observe the requirements stated in appropriate files.

Copy Protection

The Software in whole or in part may or may not be copy-protected or encrypted. However, in all cases, reselling or redistributing these files without authorization is expressly forbidden except as specifically provided for by the Owner(s) therein.

Preface

I'm sure this happens to almost everyone. When you think of the one thing that is the most precious to you, your heart begins to beat very fast. This can happen when you think of the person you love, when you hear a theme from one of your favorite composers, when a mother thinks about her unborn child, or, if you're like me, when you think about Flash motion graphics....

Flash motion graphics... To another person, this can just be a mere, random combination of three words out of the millions of words we have in our vocabulary. However, just like the Little Prince and the fox he met in the desert became beloved and unforgettable beings to each other, Flash motion graphics, to me, are words, which are very close to my heart. Continuing on with the comparison to the Little Prince, you could say that I have been tamed by Flash motion graphics.

Flash was the medium through which I was able to bring my imagination to life, while at the same time broaden the extent of my imagination. Through this, I was able to use various objects to create charming layouts and motions. It was like being a conductor of my own mini-orchestra. Everything in this world has its place and it is when these things live up to their full potential in that place that they truly shine. In Flash, I am the conductor who arranges the objects in their exact place so that they can shine through with their full potential.

Tick Tock!
One second has passed. One second...this is a measure of a very short time span. Or so I thought before working with Flash motion graphics. In Flash, one second is a very long span of time. We spend many days in order to fill up an empty space with one second of spectacular movement. During this time, we have a chance to reflect on our own abilities and there are times when this reflection causes us to fall into despair. Creating something is not an easy task. (Although, of course, the act of creation is great in itself...)

However, throughout this process, I was able to come to a very important conclusion. That is that as much as we despair, we are rewarded with that much satisfaction in the end. This is because the more thought we put into our products, the more this offers us a chance to discover something new, and hopefully, a chance to mature and grow as an artist.

So, what do we need in order to become a really good designer? There is an answer to this question. The answer is desire and time. Investing your time and effort into an avenue that interests you... isn't that the road to success in any field?

It is said that a designer's worst enemy is laziness. I reflect on this and try to put forth my entire effort into being a designer. (Although I forget from time to time...) Are you burdened by trends that seem to change very rapidly? This, however, does not mean that we can avoid them. Every time you feel burdened, say to yourself, "I am a great designer who thrives on change."

The majority of products that I have made using Flash utilize motion graphics. Filling up an empty stage and giving it an atmosphere and then modifying it to complete the scene is a very fascinating process. It allows me to approach users through one atmospherically charged media and, through visual rhythm, call out to the users to "Pay attention here!" I like this subtlety of motion graphics and the tense excitement that I feel as each of the frames that I carefully create comes alive with motion.

Have you ever spent hours just looking your work?
Have you ever fallen asleep while staring at the screen?
I really love my work. I believe that my life has become more productive as a result of my work and Flash is the friend that has made this possible.

The examples that are introduced in this book are just some of my works that I have created using this process. My private collections and commercial works are on display at my website, www.seoleuna.com. The majority of these works are those that have been created using motion graphics.

Instead of just writing down the steps that are needed to create each piece, I have also included a few passages that explain how and why I came to create it. The most important part of creating a piece of work is the process itself. It is my hope that you will approach Flash, not just to gain an understanding of the technical skills, but as a medium through which you can fully express your ideas and feelings. Your imaginations are the most important tool. I would like to believe that there are readers out there that agree with me on this point.

I want you to believe that there is a whole other universe within yourself. Flash is the tool that will bring to life our endless imaginations, and this is why I have included my own thoughts and feelings for each project in this book.

There is a saying, "Hone your skills before creating." I agree totally with this statement because I believe that in order to create you must first learn how to create. Also, by repeating this saying to yourself, you will find the other hidden meaning behind this statement: "Skills are only the tools for creation."

So, what's the most important thing? That's your imagination.

Despite the fact that the use of motion graphics is one of the most important elements of using Flash, I have always felt that it was a shame that there was no book that dealt with this matter. My first experiences with Flash had me floundering because I didn't know the easier methods for doing things and had to learn everything by trial and error. I came to write this book because I felt that there were bound to be some people out there who were like me. I really hope that this book will be of assistance, even if only a little, to those who need it and I hope that, through this book, you will be able to discover your endless possibilities.

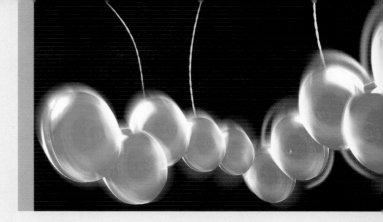

Contents

Contents

Chapter 4 - What's Wrong?

"So what's wrong with that? It doesn't matter! At least we're together!!" This statement, like a powerful rap, represents the frustrations of our heart and was poured out into a movie. Text animation and continuous bitmap images, which can be looped, were used to add velocity. In particular, specific objects were used to add continuity to the movie.

• **Interview** Eric Jordan

Chapter 5 - My Own Christmas Card

This movie, created using mask effects and composed in multi-vision form, was made paying special attention to time differential and focal point, as is the characteristic of multi-vision. Also, a carol that I sang myself was included in Flash, after undergoing some simple editing using a sound editor, and, lastly, a button was included in the movie that will respond to the actions of the mouse and cause snow to fall.

• **Interview** Matt Owens

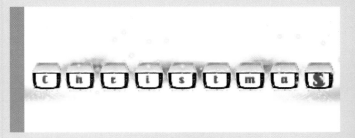

Contents

Chapter 6 - Episode from the Movie "My Sassy Girl"

The key point in this chapter was to reenact the intense dancing scene from "My Sassy Girl" as a Flash episode, within the limitations of the still screen. For the dance movements, various effects were added to symbolized bitmap images. This method allows us to create rich effects, which take up little space. In addition, an interactive element was added, which allows users to use buttons and frame labels to select the dance of their choice.

• **Interview** Jens Schmidt

Chapter 7 - The Similarity Between You & I

You? Me? Us?

We don't know each other, but we can find out how similar we are. Okay, we'll start at 50%. So, you think life is beautiful? We are about +3% similar. That's because, I think there are good and not so good aspects to life, but, overall, I think it's worth living.

It was nice meeting you.

How would it be if we could use a technique like that shown above to find out how similar we are to strangers? This was the thought process that led me to create this work. Through text field buttons in which variables are specified, these fields were made to carry out simple +, - calculations to display the percentage that changes with every question. I also added a feature that would prevent repeated calculations of the same question and an element that would immediately reveal my answer to the same question. Finally, all of the responses were taken and made into script form so that users could share their similarities with me.

Chapter 8 - Taiyup's Flash World

This chapter introduces the steps that were taken to create the homepage of Taiyup Kim, an interactive TV designer at NBC in America. taiyup.com is based on the personal essence of a toy designer. The electrifying blue background, 3D objects and the fast beat of the music are particularly eye-catching. This book describes in detail how to use Photoshop and a 3D program to create the background image and how to add text animation to Flash.

• **Interview** Taiyup Kim

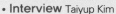

Chapter 9 - The Tracks

I took my camcorder with me to the spot that I had wandered into by chance to capture the estrangement, strangeness and the feeling of cold that enveloped me. As soon as the meaningless space captured in my camcorder began to take shape, it developed into something special. This movie, based on actual experiences, naturally blends together bitmap and vector images and uses text animation to relay the overall message. Also, action was added to prevent the overlapping of sound should the movie be set to loop repeatedly. This movie uses calm, yet tense, rhythmic visuals to display the detailed changing of emotions.

• **Interview** Todd Purgason
• **Interview** Samuel Wan

All the example source files used throughout this book are organized by chapter and included in the supplementary CD-ROM. For example, the sources used in "Chapter 4 - What's Wrong?" are saved as "What's.fla" in the Chap04 folder. These related files are mentioned in relation to each respective project and it is advised that readers refer to these files as needed.

Flash MX Motion Graphics

01 About Flash Motion Graphics

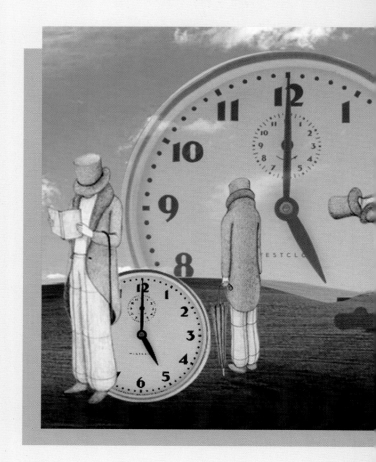

Movement and Time

The person best known for introducing "movement" into works of art is Marcel Duchamp, with his revolutionary *Bicycle Wheel* (1913). Later, in 1922 Moholy Nagy called this type of work which included linear movement, "Kinetic Art'." This form of artwork took off after the 1950's, when machinery, reflective of the Industrial Revolution which took place during this time, found its way into art. For example, the Bauhaus movement included machinery as an aesthetic representation of art, while dadaists and surrealists included machinery to criticize the civilization at that time. As a result, after 1950, "movement" came to form an intrinsic part of the works that were created.

Through this process, artists were able to introduce movement which changes with time and/or light, into still canvases. Some examples include the new method of surface slicing introduced by Picasso in order to portray 3 dimensions on a 2-dimensional canvas and the movement portrayed in Marcel Duchamp's *Nude Descending a Staircase*.

1. Kinetic: The word "kinetic" comes from the Greek word "to move" (Kinesis = movement; Kinetic = mobile) and the term "kinetic art" refers to artwork which includes movement.

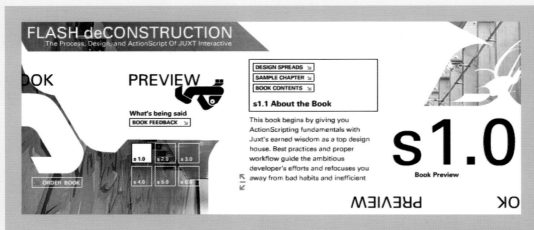

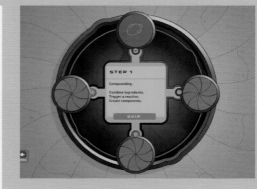

Flash Motion Graphics

"Flash Motion Graphics" are graphics that include movement and time. Our generation is one that is very familiar with movies, TV ads, music videos and other audio-visual media. We can now even witness this media on the Web. Whereas earlier Web pages were still screens limited to text, we have now leaped past these limitations and have Web canvases that can portray the full extent of our imaginations. Within this new generation of visual imagery, the program in the spotlight is Flash.

Flash is the most effective tool for creating "movement" on the Web. The reason Flash is used extensively for this purpose is because the vector-based images do not get damaged in any way when magnified or reduced. In addition, capacity problems, one of the more important points to consider on the Web, are solved through streaming technology, which allows for real-time data transmission. These reasons make Flash an ideal program, preferred above all others for use on the Web. Furthermore, one of the biggest advantages of Flash is that it allows us to add interactive elements (movements that depend on user action) for more diverse effects.

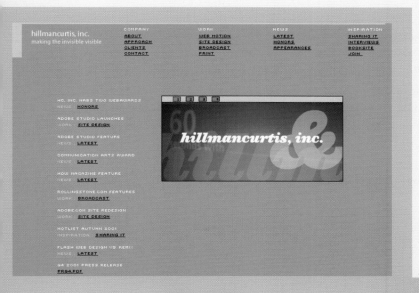

Of course, animations can be considered one part of motion graphics. However, the trend these days is to categorize a separate genre of animation called Flash animation. Here, we will only look into a limited scope of Flash Motion Graphics. (From this point on, "Flash Motion Graphics" will be referred to as "Motion Graphics.")

Conversations between people, the road you take everyday, your room... Have you ever experienced a new sensation in the things you see everyday? Unique ideas do not come from a far off land, but from common, everyday things around you. Of course you cannot transform everything you see into a work of art, but through careful attention, you should be able to snag a few ideas. It's been said that "imitation is the mother of creation." It's inevitable that different people will experience and be inspired in different ways by the same work. Although the techniques may be the same, the artist's inspiration will greatly alter the way a work is represented and the message it relays.

If you want to create your own unique style, you have to observe a lot, try a lot and feel a lot!

Web Surfing

Web surfing is another abundant source of new design ideas where we can see the works of many different artists around the world, see how far technology has progressed, and confirm the endless possibilities that are open to us. The fact that we are able to see, in real-time on our own monitors, the progress of styles from around the world is one of the greatest advantages of the Web.

However, it's a bit naive just to wander aimlessly through the Web and go wherever your mouse takes you. Because, from the countless amount of information on the Web, it is not easy to pick out the cream of the crop. This is why I would like to take the time now to introduce you to a design community that will help you attain the information you desire easily on the Web. This design community shares information with each other and works jointly on different projects while, at the same time, leading the design trends and offering the latest design news. This type of community offers a deeper level of information to those wishing to accumulate various design information and acts to create a synergistic relationship within the community.

www.surfstation.lu

www.shift.jp.org

www.threeoh.com

17

DESIGN IS KINKY (www.designiskinky.net)

"Design is kinky" is the Australia-based forum operated by Andrew Johnstone and his friend, Jade Palmer. Despite the disadvantage of location, this forum is expanding its base of recognition through its refreshing new contents and its human touch. The variety in design in this trendy site is dazzling.

K10K (www.k10k.net)

This forum, which started out with the slogan, "The Designer's Lunchbox," is now one of the most active forums around the world. The meticulous attention paid to each pixel that went into designing this site and the fast information exchange through real-time updates are the two biggest advantages of this site. In addition, the periodically updated "Issue" section is a novel area that allows users to take a peek into the experimental projects of designers. This site is operated by Mschmid and Token.

Surfstation (www.surfstation.lu)

"Surfstation," the forum based in Luxembourg, is currently the fastest growing site. This unique and trendy Web site is very pleasing to the eye.

Shift (www.shift.jp.org)

"Shift," the leader of all forums, is the site based in Sapporo, Japan and operated by Taketo Oguchi. Founded in 1996, this site is a good source of reference for observing how much Web design and technology have developed throughout the years.

Threeoh (www.threeoh.com)

"Threeoh" is a famous Web forum known for its clean design and organized contents. Through this site, users have access to unique and diverse information. The interface of this site has reduced depth so that users can access the information they want with just one click.

Various Visual Projects Seen through Different Media

We come into contact with many different media throughout our daily lives. If you have paid careful attention to MTV, TV ads and music videos, you have already acquired a great foundation of design sources.

The style of Flash motion graphics has been largely influenced by such media, which is presented to the designer as a finished product. Of course, Flash graphics on the Web also, in turn, influence TV. Although the media and the tools they use may be different, both are largely affected by one another.

A while ago, I saw *Charlie's Angels* and *The Mummy 2* and was greatly surprised. Both movies used Flash to create the movie titles. In *Charlie's Angels,* large sliced surfaces and colors were animated, characteristic of Flash vector graphics, and in *The Mummy 2,* the cast credits were created using text animation, a style used in Flash.

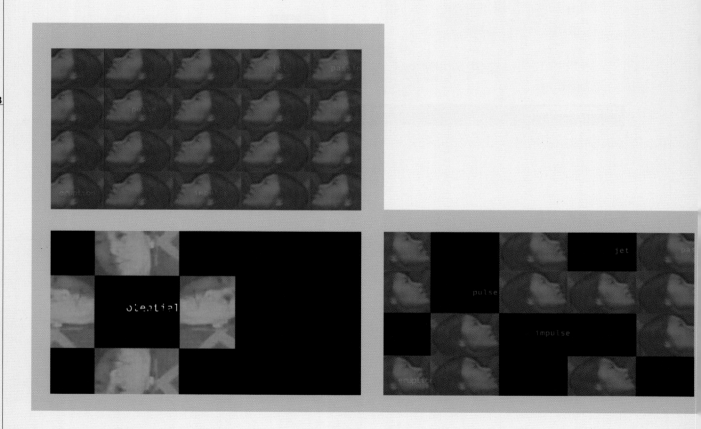

Of course it's possible that these two just happened to use the same method of representation. However, the fact that Flash offers new methods of representation to other media cannot be denied. And, in reality, these kinds of products that we come into contact with are a great source of inspiration to our own actual work.

Several years ago, after seeing the movie, *Seven,* I felt a chill throughout my entire body. The old and faded letters that seem to jump out from the screen, the sharp sounds that stimulated my auditory nerves, the development of the picture that created a tense excitement and the eerie fascination that seemed to pull the viewer in to the screen... these were not simply factors that had been inserted into the movie. Rather, these factors were the movie itself. (The audio-visual for the movie *Seven* can be seen at http:// www.imaginaryforces.com.) Afterwards, I found out that the genius behind this was Kyle Cooper, a deified pioneer who opened a new avenue of possibility into this field. His work not only expands the scope of our imaginations, but shows us the endless possibilities that are available to the field of computer graphics. This is probably the reason why his work is a source of inspiration to many and the reason why it is studied closely by designers around the world.

After being inspired by the movie, *Seven,* I decided to try my hand at creating "grunge" graphic. I thought of the characters as living organisms and wanted to create a project in which the letters would shake violently upon stimulation, combust and then disappear as it scratches down the wall.

A project in which the faded and rough texture was recreated using Flash

I named this feeling "fever" and used it in one of my projects. This is the result of using this rough texture and irregular text as elements in one of my projects. (This is saved as "fever.swf" in the supplementary CD or can be seen at http://www.seoleuna .com/.)

Life Experiences

As I mentioned before, although Web surfing and observing other visual graphics are important, the real source of inspiration comes from the things around us.

Could it be possible that we have missed the infinite sources that nature provides us with? Have you ever felt a sense of wonderment in the way an insect moves? Or in the vaguely visible outlines of people seen through a dense fog? Did you ever find joy in the sound of footsteps or in the sound of a car engine? Have you ever looked up into the heavens and thought of it as a wonderful graphic?

If your sense of imagination is stimulated by the seemingly ordinary things that you see everyday, then you have an infinite foundation of inspiration for your work.

I sometimes take my camcorder and start filming at random the world around me and it is through these clips that I see things that I have failed to notice before. When the world around us is moved onto the screen, even the seemingly ordinary aspects of life become extraordinary.

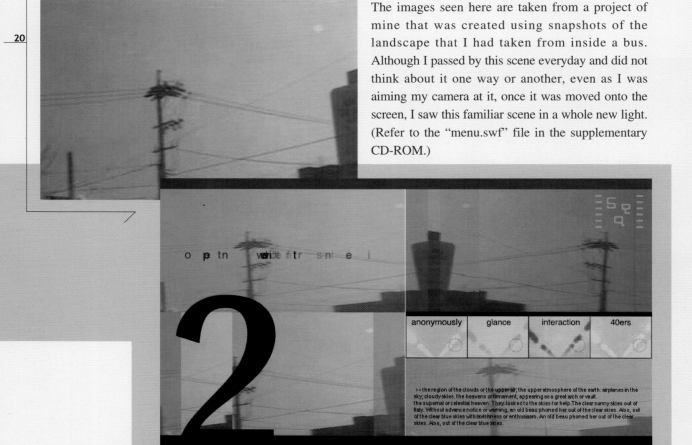

The images seen here are taken from a project of mine that was created using snapshots of the landscape that I had taken from inside a bus. Although I passed by this scene everyday and did not think about it one way or another, even as I was aiming my camera at it, once it was moved onto the screen, I saw this familiar scene in a whole new light. (Refer to the "menu.swf" file in the supplementary CD-ROM.)

I want to point out another example. It was one lazy winter afternoon and I had nothing to do. The fierce winds had frozen solid the world outside and stifled any desire I had to leave my house. However, with nothing else to do, I turned on the computer and decided to convert the atmosphere of the day into another project.

"What did I do today? I slept, drank water, meditated... Will I remember today 3 days from now?" Even such a simple experience can serve as a source for a project. The originality of the project is found in its very simplicity. (Refer to the "jan5.swf" file in the supplementary CD-ROM.)

I believe that if we pay just the least bit of attention, the world around us is overflowing with potential sources. Everyday life that is ignored by other people can be a fountainhead of inspiration for those who seek it.

It is my hope that you and I will develop the ability to see the world around us in a different light.

Motion Graphic Techniques

I just opened Flash in order to make a 15-second movie. Do you feel a sense of despair from staring at the vast empty canvas of the monitor? Then, the things you need to get ready before starting the actual work and the things you need to consider before and after you finish working are...what?

Here, I will organize the entire process of motion graphics and techniques based on my past experiences.

The process of creating motion graphics can be divided into the following 5 categories:

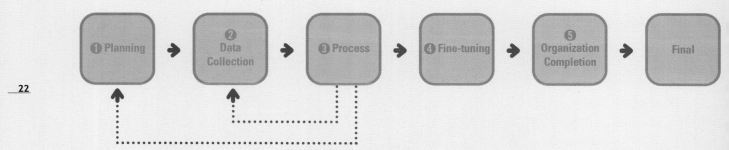

Planning

This is the step where you think about the type of project you want to create and draw a sketch in your head. The important thing in this step is to think about the message that you want to relay and then create the respective atmosphere. For example, if you want to create a movie that introduces a modern art gallery, you need to decide on colors that will reflect the sophisticated and clean lines of the subject matter and think about the main copy that will relay the implications of the movie. In addition, this step requires you to set up the mood of the movie. In the case of our example, a continuous progression of little changes within a calm and elegant tranquility will be appropriate. In this way, the planning step involves thinking about the overall process in your mind or through a sketch.

It is also a good idea to organize your thoughts and/or sketches in a storyboard, especially if you are working on a team or for a client. Sharing your ideas with those you are working with is important for a smoothly running operation. Of course, your final result might be slightly different from the ideas organized on your storyboard. This is only because there are bound to be differences between your imagination and the actual outcome. In this instance, it is important and necessary to hold meetings in which you and your teammates will be able to discuss the appropriate direction for your work. This feedback is represented by the dotted arrow that moves from the "Process" step back to the "Planning" step in the figure on the previous page.

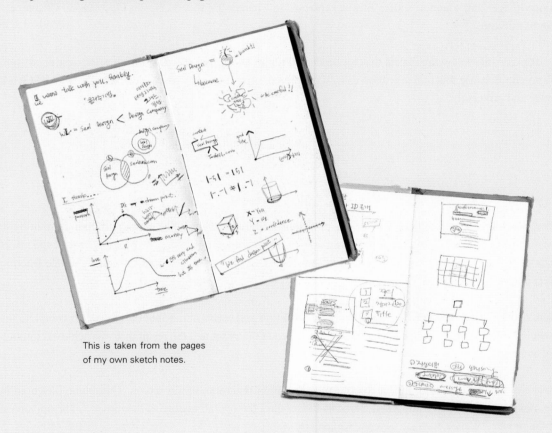

This is taken from the pages
of my own sketch notes.

The planning step will become the skeleton for the entire operation. It is important to grasp the proper direction at this point because unstable planning will lead to a weak result.

Data Collection

This is the step where we collect and organize the data needed to carry out the plans for our movie. For example, you will have to request data in order to receive the bitmap images that you need and, at times, you will have to go out and collect the images yourself. For the loop bitmap images I frequently use for continuous scenes, after filming the scenes myself, I go through several steps in order to organize my source files. This is the series of steps that is involved in data collection. We need to optimize the source files, organized according to our plan, so that they can be used directly within the movie. (The process for using bitmap images and sound as source files is explained in Chapter 2 - Video Clips in Flash and in Chapter 3 - Sounds in Flash.)

For example, the following is data that was collected for an interactive movie showing a 360-degree rotation of a room. Because this movie will be using a panorama form, it is important to fix the focal point and work slowly and efficiently.

After these images are scanned, we need to use Photoshop, or another image editing program, to join these images together. The key is to link the pictures together as smoothly as possible because each of them was taken at slightly different angles. In addition, we need to correct the colors and undergo a simple filtering effect in order to produce richer colors.

Then, action scripts are added to the source files in Flash and made into a motion graphic to complete the movie. The following shows the data that was collected at the onset and the result that was achieved through trial and error.

Users will be able to use the mouse to observe each part of this room in this movie. The source files used in this movie are particularly important elements that control the overall quality of the movie. (The homepage for the movie, "Wanee & Junah": www.wnj.co.kr)

Each of the pictures, taken at slightly different angles, have been arranged haphazardly.

After linking together the pictures in Photoshop and correcting the color.

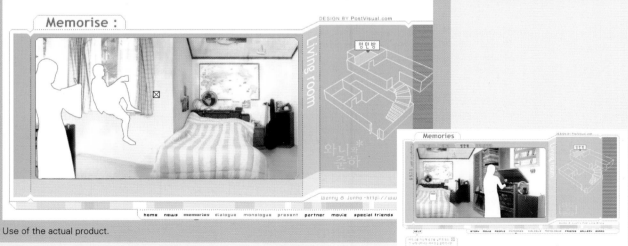

Use of the actual product.

Investigating Vector and Bitmap Images

Vector images are images where each line, surface and point are mathematically calculated and stored. There is no change in the image information or capacity when magnifying and reducing because the image is represented by the endpoints of each line. Flash is a program that uses such vectors and, therefore, Flash files are relatively smaller in size and can be altered effectively.

In contrast, bitmap images arrange color information on a grid pattern. The smallest unit of such color information is called a pixel. These pixels then come together to form one image. Upon magnifying the image, each of these pixels becomes apparent. We can compare the differences in these two types of images by looking at the images below.

Bitmap Image – Magnifying this image shows a step-like pattern.

Vector Image – There is no change to the image even upon magnification.

Flash supports vector drawing, but, at times, bitmap images can be loaded for use.

	Bitmap Images	Vector Images
Advantages	When used appropriately, bitmap images can be used to create scenes with more density than can be created using vector images alone.	Small capacity files that offer clean images upon magnifying and reducing.
Disadvantages	Comparatively larger file sizes and the image breaks up upon magnifying and reducing.	Can only be used to handle simple images. File sizes become larger than bitmap images when handling more complex images, such as pictures.

Taking these factors into consideration, you will be able to apply vector or bitmap images depending on the situation.

Process

After planning and gathering the necessary data, we now need to put all these things together on the canvas. It goes without saying that this and the following step, "Fine-tuning," are the most important steps in motion graphics. The planning and the actual work can be very different and the presence of many variables can be slightly confusing.

You are the producer in charge of putting all of these things together. Everything lies in your hands. Even though the planning and the script may be the same, the results can differ greatly depending on the producer who puts it all together. For each movement that gets added into each frame, there are many things to consider. The examples in this book show how to deal with each of these situations and the method that I selected. Knowing which method is best for each situation is a difficult decision you have to make, but it is what makes motion graphics fun. The following are the things you need to consider during this step.

Arranging the Main Character, Supporting Actors and Extras

There are many elements that make up a movie. However, an organized movie never loses its focus. In order for all the many factors to appear organized and put together you must give each element its own role, just like in a movie where we have the main character, the supporting actors and extras and close and long shots.

In making a movie, I always arrange the elements to have 1 point, 2 point, 3 point roles and fit this into the flow of the movie. When viewers see my movie, they are left with the feeling of having seen a lot, yet not having seen enough. This feeling is what grabs the viewer's attention. However, the main message of the movie is relayed through the main character. Of course, the movie will not be fun if the same method is used in the same way from beginning to end. You need to add rhythm to the entire movie, by sometimes using only the main character, the supporting actors or the extras.

This method is necessary if you want to create a richer movie. Keeping in mind this method, think back to some of your favorite motion graphics. You will come to realize that many motion graphics utilize this method. Who will be the star in the next example? (Refer to the "tracks.swf" file in the supplementary CD-ROM.)

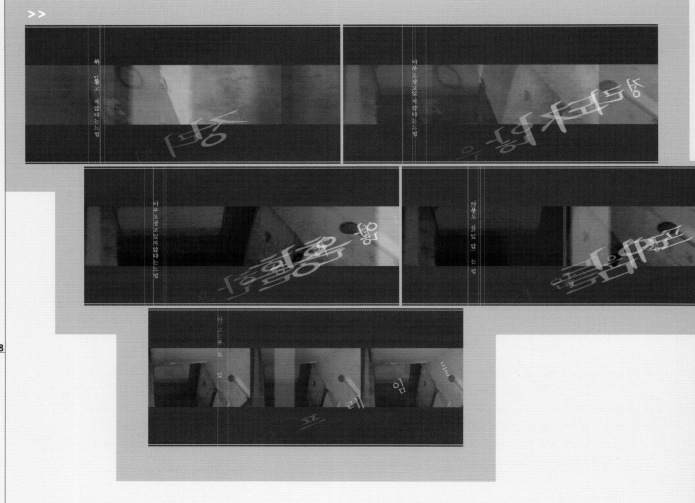

The next "star" is text animation. The main character acts to grab the viewer's attention by having the most movement, being the largest or by having the largest color variation.

The supporting actor in this screen is the moving image in the background and the extras are the white lines and the surface, which are barely moving, in the corners of the screen. Of course, these roles can be changed at any time. The extras can become the main character and the main character can become the supporting actor. What matters most is how these roles are arranged and how naturally they appear at each moment in time.

The important thing here is harmony. How these elements fit together is what will determine the quality of your end product.

Always Consider the Viewer's Point of View.

This ties in with what we were discussing before about prolonging the movie. When you make a movie, it is important to capture the viewer's gaze. Of course, in the previous example, the main character will act to grab the viewer's attention. However, there are other methods available. We can use supporting lines or use effects that stimulate the viewer's attention. In particular, in between scene transitions it is important that the scenes do not abruptly end, but change smoothly. (For example, instead of using the common "fade in/out" method, you could think of another way to make scene transitions more dynamic....)

It is very important to grab hold of the viewer's attention and to not let it wander. For example, in the following movie, the circular shape acts to entice the viewer's attention throughout the entire movie. Using "Zoom" within the screen and directly specifying the point at which the zoom should stop is used to continue the flow of the movie. More details can be found in Chapter 4 "What's Wrong."

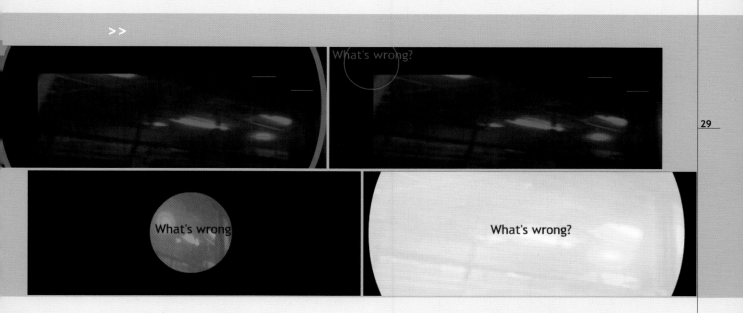

In addition, as seen in the following movie, the black rectangle, seen before the text animation, acts to hold the attention of the viewer. Drastic changes in color and movement are the instruments which entice the viewer's attention. (Refer to Chapter 5 "My Own Christmas Card.")

There are countless other things to consider and methods that can be used in making a movie, which cannot all be mentioned here. A portion of these other methods and considerations will be explained in the examples throughout this book. The others, I believe, you will encounter through your many experiences.

Fine-Tuning

The following step is closely related to the previous step. Here we modify portions of the movie to fine-tune the rhythm of the entire movie. This step is applied to developing movies and movies that are arranged in parallel. We'll look at the overall picture of the movie and add or delete elements to maintain the flow.

Adding dynamism and considering scene transitions and movements are what largely tie the movie together. This process can be applied during the actual making of the movie or in the final inspection steps.

Here are the following points that we need to consider in this step:

Adjusting Movements

Adjusting the stress in the movie not only helps to more strongly relay the message of the movie, but allows viewers to feel the rhythm. This can be thought of as adding the element of elasticity to the movie. In other words, tenser moments in the movie are drawn tighter and lighter moments are more relaxed. The arrangement of these elements is involved in this step.

For example, some movies can be made that start out weak in the beginning and pick up speed along the way, with faster scene transitions and color changes, to culminate in a climactic last scene. However, other movies can be moved away from the parallel structure and progress through slight stress adjustments and changes in scene. The important thing to remember is to create rhythm within the overall movie structure.

Don't Forget Tension.

The minute that a movie begins to lose some tension, viewers will begin to lose interest. The minute viewers begin to lose interest their attention begins to wander. By maintaining unity and a certain amount of tension within that unity, you will be able to hold the viewer's attention.

For example, the CD-ROM contains a motion graphic entitled "tracks.swf" which is arranged in parallel form. After I first made this movie, I felt that there was something missing. Of course the movie had transition, but I felt the flow to be too consistent from beginning to end. Therefore, I added some tempo throughout the movie; some images were made to move slowly at first and then suddenly move quickly to their positions and others were zoomed in on rapidly before moving back to their original form.

These adjustments changed the rhythm of the entire movie and added structure and tension. In this way, polishing your final movie requires that you watch your movies over and over again and modify them frame-by-frame. This step requires you to consider which areas can be deleted and which areas need to be stronger or weaker. This will allow you to achieve a more polished and satisfactory result.

Organization

Finally, in order for the movie created in this way to be placed on the Web, it must be optimized. This step, the final step in motion graphics, means tending to the inner elements of the movie. All of the movies that we create are made with the intention of placing them on the Web. What this means is that our movies must be optimized in terms of capacity, size and speed, and we must consider how all of these elements can be effectively adjusted.

Optimizing the Movie

One of the disadvantages of Flash movies is that they can appear differently on each viewer's computer. In other words, the Flash movie will play differently depending on the speed of the viewer's CPU. The movie that was optimized to 30 frames/second on your computer might appear at a reduced speed on someone else's computer.

Let's try playing the movie in Flash. We can see that the frames per second value changes from time to time. This means that the CPU speed cannot follow the speed to which we have configured our movie. Therefore, we need to undergo a process of dispersing or adjusting this effectively.

In order to have others view your movie as you intended, you need to unburden the file and remove all possible hurdles in arranging the movements.

The following are factors, which I have experienced, that lower the speed of Flash movies:

- ➡ Motion-tweening symbolized bitmap images or objects with many surfaces.
- ➡ Using symbolized bitmap images to which an alpha value has been applied. (In particular, the speed is reduced further in motion-tweening in which the opacity (alpha value) changes.)
- ➡ When objects that contain gradiation are used or when they are tweened.
- ➡ When objects with complex surfaces are shape-tweened.
- ➡ Using simultaneous movements.

As mentioned above, there are many factors which can lower the speed of movies. Therefore, in order to more effectively manage movies, we must disperse the movements and change these elements to optimize the file to fit the character of the movie. There is no one best way of doing this. It's important that you adjust and tune the movie to fit the message and the mood that you are trying to relay. In addition, in this last step, you must undergo the process of optimizing your movie in terms of file size. This includes making the final adjustments to the images and sound files used in your movie.

The following are things that you should keep in mind as you make the final touches to your movie.

Readjusting the Size of Bitmap Images.

Bitmap images are very big and you will see that a file size different from the one when you first loaded Flash, will appear. If the second file is smaller than the file size of the one first loaded, it's best to adjust the size and then load it again and delete the previous file. However, you must first organize all the unnecessary images. If you are only going to be using portions of the movie, it's best to load and trim only the portions you are going to use.

Let me explain further using an example.
I imported the image that I collected during the "Data Collection" step into Flash.

However, I will only be using a portion of this image for the actual movie.

Therefore, after cutting out the necessary portion in Photoshop, I imported that portion back into Flash. Because we have deleted unnecessary portions of the image, the file size will be much smaller. Of course, in deleting the previous cut, we replaced it with the newer cut.

As follows, in the final step, we must cut out only the portions we wish to use.

The image used in the actual movie.

The image collected during the "Data Collection" step.

Applying Individual Compression to Bitmap Images · · · · ·

Images handled in this way, depending on use frequency and/or character, must be individually compressed. For images that play an important role in the movie, the compression rate is set to low for better image resolution. For all other instances, the image compression is set to high. This compression is adjusted in the Bitmap Properties window in the library.

Bitmap icon

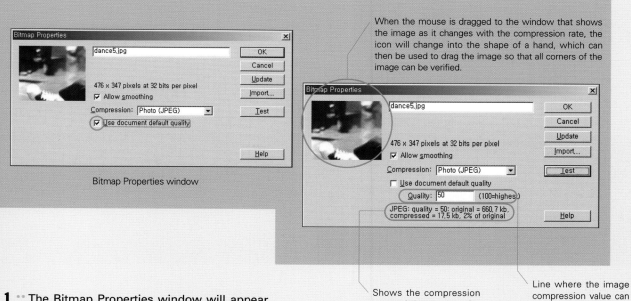

Bitmap Properties window

When the mouse is dragged to the window that shows the image as it changes with the compression rate, the icon will change into the shape of a hand, which can then be used to drag the image so that all corners of the image can be verified.

Shows the compression rate and the resultant file capacity.

Line where the image compression value can be entered.

1 · · The Bitmap Properties window will appear when the bitmap image icon is double-clicked. For JPEG images, the default is set to "Use document default quality." This means that the compression rate specified in [File]-[Publish Settings] will be applied uniformly to all images. Because we want to apply different compression rates to different images, we deselect this option.

2 · · You should see a box named "Quality" in which the compression rate can be entered manually. Entering the desired value here and pressing the "Test" button allows us to preview the image and the resultant file capacity. An optimal value should be selected that results in an optimal file size and quality.

Using the "Test Movie" Feature

Flash contains a feature called "Test Movie" that allows us to see a preview of the movie. This feature is very useful for adjusting file capacity or for putting together a loading movie. Not only can we obtain information on various "swf" files, we can easily verify if the movie we are making now is in "swf" format. Without a doubt, this is one feature that is essential in creating Flash movies.

In order to see which section takes up the most space and to see if any unnecessary segments have been added, the streaming graph in "Test Movie" mode is very useful. This graph shows us the size per frame allowing us to check which areas are overly large and which areas can be deleted. We can enter "Test Movie" mode by selecting [Control]-[Test Movie] or by using the shortcut keys (Ctrl + Enter , ⌘ + Enter).

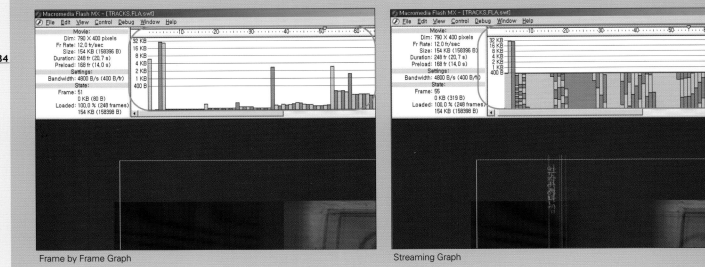

Frame by Frame Graph   Streaming Graph

■ Data Graph

The "Test Movie" mode offers two bar graphs, "Streaming Graph" and "Frame by Frame Graph," that show the transmission capacity. These graphs allow movie producers to see the optimization status of the movie in one glance. As we can see in the images above, the "Frame by Frame Graph" is a graph that shows data per frame and the "Streaming Graph" is a graph that shows if the data in each frame has been distributed properly.

The settings for this example are configured to received 2.4k/sec meaning that the breadth of substitution for each frame is 200 bites. (The transmission rate per second can be configured in the [Debug] menu.) Therefore, there is a red line on the graph at 200 bites, meaning that everything below this line will run without delay. However, for frames that surpass this breadth, the movie will stop momentarily and resume once the specified capacity has been downloaded.

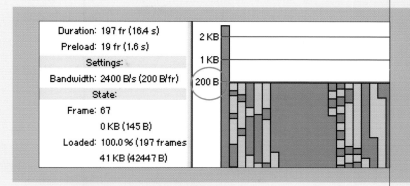

When the movie is set to "Streaming," as the current movie is being transmitted, it will continue to load the upcoming data to disperse the file capacity. Also, through this "Streaming Graph," we can see how movies on the Web are transmitted and shown and how long the movie will take to load.

35

tip
∨
∨

What is Substitution Breadth?

The substitution breadth refers to the amount of data that can be received per second on the Web. In other words, if the substitution breadth is 2.4kb/sec, in a movie that transmits 12 frames/sec, it receives 200 bites/sec. This substitution breadth value can be changed in the "Test Movie" mode by selecting [Debug]-[Customize].

■ Streaming Test

In the "Test Movie" mode, we can test how the actual movie will appear on the Web. This is done by selecting [View]-[Show Streaming]. When this option is selected, the transmission rate per second that was configured in the [Debug] menu will be applied to show us an exact rendition of the movie.

The amount transmitted is represented by the green bar seen in the frame header of the graph. If the movie data exceeds the substitution breadth, this green bar will pause momentarily. This means that the movie will stop momentarily until all the movie data is received.

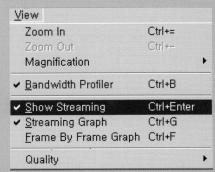

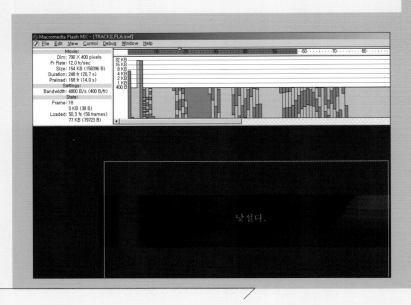

This movie data is useful for dispersing the file capacity of the movie. For example, if there is too much data in frame 10 causing the movie to pause, we can verify and reduce the amount of data in this frame. Graphs that are too high represent frames that require some modification in capacity.

Also, if the "if frame is loaded" action is used when using the streaming graph, we can calculate at which point (*i.e.* after which frame is loaded) the movie will be played. For example, if a movie consists of a total of 100 frames, we can have the movie start playing after all 100 frames have been loaded or after only 70 frames have been loaded. We can do this because after 70 frames have been loaded, the remaining 30 frames will be loaded during the time the movie is played.

Using the "Test Movie" mode allows us to see at one glance the entire capacity structure of the movie. This is useful in removing unnecessary loads and for effectively distributing the capacity.

The fundamental reason why we undergo this organization and optimization stage in this final step is because we want to offer the viewer a movie that is as close as possible to the state in which we created it. If you do not want all the hard work that you have put into the previous steps to go to waste, this last step requires your utmost attention.

Those Who Are Not Loved Wither Away

There was once a point in time when I did not turn on the computer for two months. I was so busy that I did not have the time to even turn on my computer. Then, one day, something came up for which I needed the computer and something was very wrong with the system, which had been running perfectly up until this point. The power would not even turn on. What had happened in the last two months?

I reached my own conclusion.

My computer, which I had ignored for two months, was now very angry with me... *^^*
I know this sounds rather ridiculous, but the reason I mention this is because creating a truly exceptional piece of work requires much love and attention.

"Love the work that you do."

Put your all into each frame and arrange each element so that its full potential will shine through. A truly exceptional piece of work only comes from endless effort on your part.

Flash MX
Motion Graphics

James Widegren

www.threeoh.com

THREE.OH is a conduit for all those interested in communications arts. Our editorial focus is the relationship between the various creative disciplines and design [in its broadest sense] and furthermore, their relationship to the medium of the World-Wide Web.

This site is intended to act as a gateway to the work of other designers, musicians, architects, filmmakers and photographers.

We wish to explore concepts, inspire artistic experimentation and encourage creative growth within our audience. We instigate critical dialogues with other talented creatives in order to share our passion for communication design in all its forms. Our primary goal is to inform, provoke and motivate the creative audience we cater to by opening up public forums for discussion, both within the web-design community and beyond.

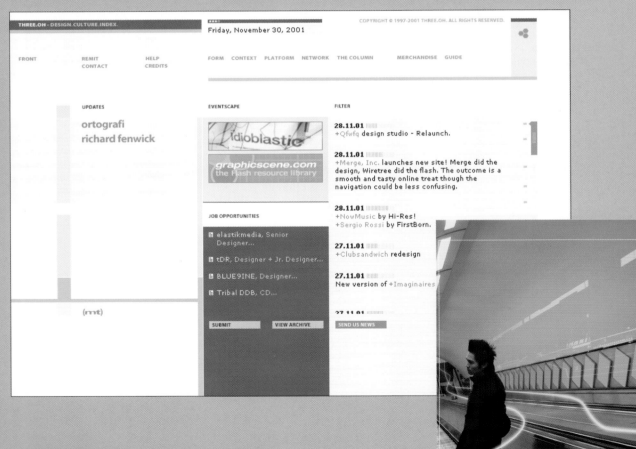

James Widegre

Taketo Oguchi

www.shift.jp.org

1. What's your purpose in operating the site?

Its goal is to introduce the hidden talents worldwide in the vast cyber space. Being a cross point for the creators in Japan and the rest of the world, this is where Shift receives, selects, and then edits what we believe to be the most interesting sites on the cutting edge of the net to provide you with a new perspective today.

2. Please, tell me a distinctive feature of your site, compared with other design communities?

We cover not only issues in design area but also ones in the wider culture. That is our strength.

3. If you recommend a section in your site...?

Info-World would be good. It has news by correspondents from all over the world.

Copyright © 1997-2001 SHIFT (Japan) / Shift Production, Ltd. All Rights Reserved.

Taketo Oguchi

Flash MX Motion Graphics

02. Video Clips in Flash

The Role of Video in Flash

The use of bitmap images and vector graphics in our work is an essential component of using motion graphics.

Flash is a vector-based program. That is why, in the beginning, most of the work involved vectors. Of course, bitmap images were also used, but these were used only to express that which could not be shown using vector images and were merely descriptive. However, more and more projects that effectively utilized both vector and bitmap images started to appear. This was done to make up for the disadvantages of vector graphics and became an important technique in Flash.

Creative Flash sites using vector graphics as the main element

www.e3direktiv.com (Basic version)

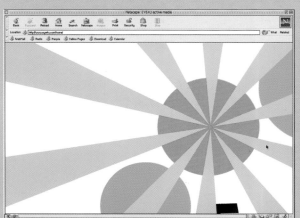
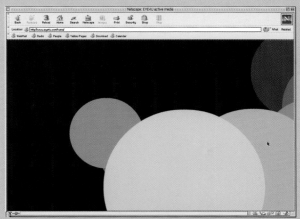

www.eye4u.com

Expression on the Web is always in inverse proportion to remaining file capacity. This is why we hesitate to use several pages of bitmap images. In particular, for continuous motions, we need more than 20 frames per second and this is overly excessive for Flash. As always, the matter of file capacity becomes our greatest hurdle.

However, we can overcome these disadvantages by using looped cuts. Using looped cuts, which continue naturally from start to finish, several repetitions can be shown without interruption and we can make them into symbols to alleviate the tediousness that can come from continuously repeating frames. Because one action uses less than 10 cuts, we can have the maximum effect for the minimum file capacity.

43

The blinking scene of
cyber singer "Lucia"

I use this type of continuous action bitmap frequently in my work and I receive many questions from users on how to put video clips into Flash, how to optimize them and how to utilize them in movies. Here, I will talk about how to use video clips in Flash.

In addition, we will learn more about the video import feature, new to Flash MX, how to use this new feature more effectively and we will discuss compression rates.

First, we will learn how to export a continuous still cut of a video capture and import it into Flash using the steps outlined here. Of course, there are many other ways, but I've outlined the method that I use most frequently.

- Video captures and export (in Premiere)
- Image editing and revision (in Photoshop)
- Optimizing images in Flash
- Using the video clip

Video Capture and Export (In Premiere)

In order to use a portion of the movie we filmed using a camcorder in Flash, we must first convert the image into a digital file. Here, we will capture the movie, filmed using DV, in Premiere, an AV editing program, and learn how to prepare this to be used in Flash. Before capturing, you must first verify if the movie capture board on your computer is configured properly and that the cables are connected properly. Reception through FireWire terminals will ensure good resolution. You should try to receive the transmission that will offer the best resolution possible, for the better the original image is, the better the compressed image will be.

Video Clip Capturing Methods

There are 4 different types of video clip capturing methods.

Batch Capture

If you have digital control equipment, you can divide the video source into several clips and then capture them all at once. In order to use Batch Capture, you must first create a Batch List, which will show the portions we wish to capture. For example, if we want to capture a movie of a marathon race, we can flip through the movie from the beginning and list the portions we wish to capture in the Batch List (here, we wish to capture the start of the race, the return points and the finish line). Then, when we start Batch Capture, it will capture only those portions listed in the Batch List. This method is useful for capturing the essential points of an otherwise very long movie.

Movie Capture

This is the most basic capturing method in which we select the portions for capture while watching the movie. Because the majority of sources that are used in Flash are rather simple, Batch Capture is not always necessary. For shorter video clips, Movie Capture is the more convenient method.

Stop Motion

This method allows us to capture video clips as still screens. It also allows us to capture stills at fixed time intervals or by selecting only the cuts we want.

Audio Capture

Audio captures are not supported by Premiere itself and we must use an external program (Sound Forge, Sound Edit, Windows recorder, etc.) to capture sound.

tip

The term "device controller" refers to an external deck (digital camcorder or other such equipment), connected automatically to the computer and having the keyboard or mouse used to control the movie in Premiere. For example, let's suppose that we used the mouse to push the Rewind button in Premiere. When we do this, the source tape in the digital camcorder will rewind at the same time, which is much easier than controlling the external deck directly. This ability to control external decks from within a program is referred to as a device controller.

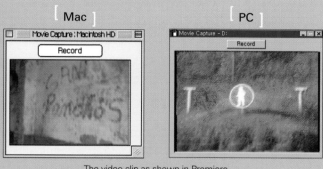

The video clip as shown in Premiere

Capturing

Movie Capture

Let's look now at the most basic capturing method, Movie Capture, for both Mac and PC environments.

1 Select [File]-[Capture]-[Movie Capture].

2 Start running the connected camcorder. When the video clip that we wish to capture appears, press the [Record] button. To stop the capture, press the Esc key or click on the mouse.

3 When the capture is complete, the information window of the captured clip, saved as a temporary file on the canvas, will appear together with the clip.

4 Select [File]-[Save] to save the capture. Saving files as avi, mov and mpg allows them to be imported into Flash directly.

45

Clip information window

Clip window

Exporting Movie Captures as Continuous Still Bitmap Cuts

In Flash 5, we were only allowed to import and export mov files. However, in Flash MX, we are now able to import as avi, mpg and mov files and export as swf files. In addition, we are now able to play these files in any system, be it MAC or PC, that has a Flash MX player. Also, imported video clips can be saved as symbols for re-editing and applying different effects in Flash to take us beyond the limitations of mere motion graphics. However, no matter how high the compression rate of these video clips, the file sizes are too much for Flash. Therefore, it is more effective, in terms of file size, to use shorter video clips or looped bitmap images. We will look at both instances here.

First, we will look at how to convert movie captures into still cuts. If you want to create a continuous motion, all you have to do is fit several still cuts into the flow of the movie. We will divide one action into several still cuts and then link them back together again to create a realistic and natural action. In most cases, 3-7 stills are used for a simple action. For example, for an eye-blinking sequence, 3-4 stills, at the very least, are needed.

Exporting Movie Files as Continuous Still Cuts] · · · ·

1 ** Use the [File]-[Export]-[Frame] command to export the desired frame as a still cut.

2 ** After verifying the current settings in the [Export Still Frame] dialogue box, press the [Settings...] button to change the next option.

3 ** We must specify the export file format in the [Export Still Frame] dialogue box. File formats which can be used in both PC and Mac, are GIF, TIFF and Targa. Here, we will use TIFF. Selecting the "Open when finished" option in General Settings, the still cut will open in the clip window when export is complete. This option can be selected as needed.

4 ** After configuring the settings in the [Export Still Frame Settings] dialogue box, press the [OK] button.

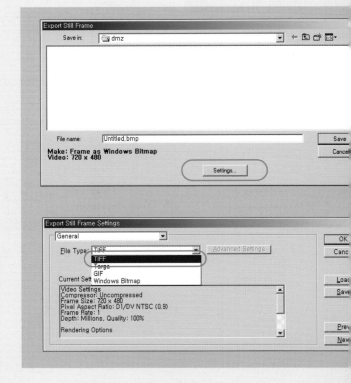

5 You will be taken back to the [Export Still Frame] window. Enter the file name and then press [OK].

6 Because we selected the "Open when finished" option, the captured file will appear in the clip window.

7 In order to stop the looped action, using the same method, export several cuts while using the mouse to adjust the running of the movie. This method is useful for selecting the desired scenes from a movie file and converting them into still cuts.

The loading of the captured file in the clip window

In the method illustrated above, we have to manually save one cut at a time and, consequently, we have a lot of restrictions. Premiere has a feature which allows still cuts of the move to be exported at fixed time intervals, and this is useful for when we need to capture several pages of looped cuts in a short amount of time. In addition, because this method automatically creates a fixed time interval between cuts, it results in a more natural looped image than if we had adjusted this interval manually. In other words, this means that we can export a 1-minute movie at 1 cut per second for a total of 60 still cuts. This is the method of choice for converting a natural looped cut from a movie file into a still cut.

Exporting a Movie File into a Still Cut at a Fixed Time Interval

1 •• First, we need to open the movie file that we want to export as a still image. Select [File]-[Export]-[Movie]. We need to determine where we will save the exported image. In this example, because we will be exporting several looped cuts, we will make a new folder.

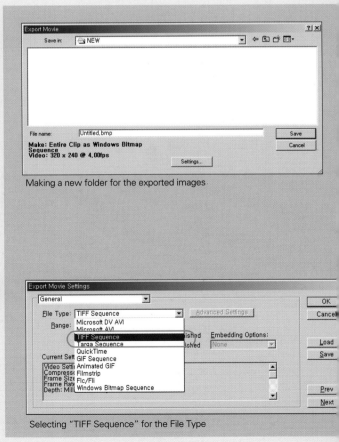

Making a new folder for the exported images

2 •• Click the [Settings...] button to open the [Export Movie Settings] dialogue box. We need to select the File Type. Here, we will select "TIFF Sequence," which can be used in both Mac and PCs.

Selecting "TIFF Sequence" for the File Type

Changing from "General Settings" to "Video."

3 ** Now we need to adjust the time interval for the movie still capture. This can be done in "Video." We will configure the movie to be captured at 3 frames per second.

Setting the Frame Rate to 3 frames per second.

4 ** Returning to the [Export Movie Settings] dialogue box, we can see "Frame Rate:3.00" in the Current Settings box.

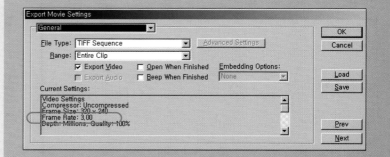

5 When the configurations have been made, click the [OK] button. Then, press [OK] in the "Save" box that appears to start the capture.

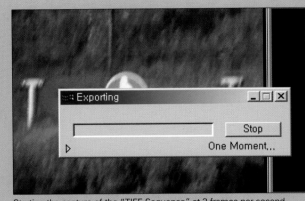

Starting the capture of the "TIFF Sequence" at 3 frames per second

6 The following still files will appear in the specified folder. These still cuts can now be imported directly into Flash or can be used after undergoing simple revisions in an image-editing program.

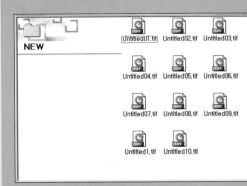

TIFF files created at fixed time intervals

tip >>

Capturing Still Cuts Using the Screen Capture Method.

Among the methods available for capturing movie files as still cuts is the method used for capturing the computer screen itself. For Mac, we use the shortcut key Shift + ⌘ + 3 and for PC, we use the Print Screen key.

However, because we cannot conduct a continuous capture in PCs, we first need to save the one cut that we captured in an image-editing program, like Photoshop or Paintshop, capture it again and then repeat this step.

Image Editing and Revision (In Photoshop)

Images that have been captured again as still cuts need to undergo a simple revision, including cutting out unnecessary images, adjusting image color tones, specifying the image file format, etc., in an editing program before they can be loaded into Flash. Of course, at times, additional image work is also done.

In addition, before the image can be loaded into Flash, the file format (JPG, GIF, PNG) must be specified first. The format that is chosen depends on the status of the image.

After Specifying an Appropriate Resolution, Only the Necessary Portions Are Trimmed.

Trimming an image for presentation on the Web is the same as setting how it appears on the monitor. The standard resolution of monitors is 72ppi and we will match the image resolution to this. It is a good idea to verify the resolution for images that have been scanned or downloaded. In Photoshop, we can set the resolution to 72ppi by selecting [Image]-[Image size].

We must also crop images leaving behind only the portions we are going to use. Unnecessary images increase the file size and are the greatest hurdles to achieving optimized movies. To crop images, select the Crop Tool(🔲)from the toolbar and press the (Enter) key leaving behind only the necessary portions of the image.

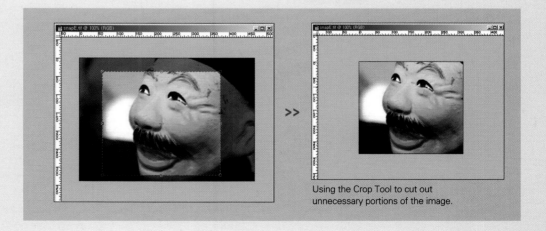

Using the Crop Tool to cut out
unnecessary portions of the image.

In the actual making of the movie, however, there comes times when, contrary to your initial plans, you do not use all of the images that you have imported or you must increase/reduce the size of these images. This is why we need to revise the images in an image-editing program before importing them into Flash. (When revising images, it is a good idea to delete the older images so you do not get confused.)

Adjusting Color, Contrast and Brightness

In this step, we correct images and add filter effects as necessary. You can use the method that you normally use for color revision, but I usually use [Image]-[Level], [Image]-[Curve], [Image]-[Adjust]-[Brightness/Contrast] or [Image]-[Adjust]-[Color Balance] to adjust image color and to get rid of excess noise.

The important thing is that the images must be in the most optimal condition before loading into Flash. A good source image will result in a good compressed image.

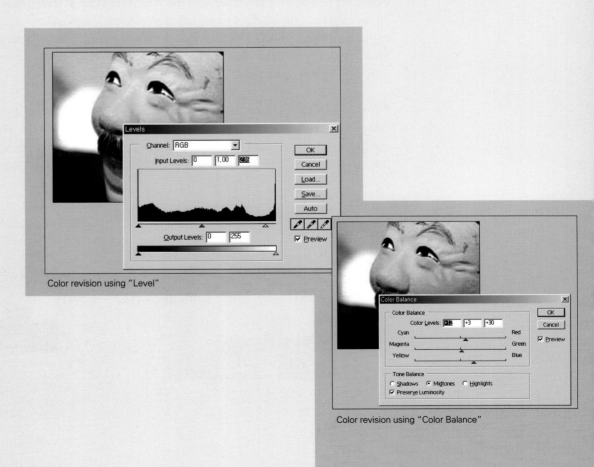

Color revision using "Level"

Color revision using "Color Balance"

52

Saving as JPG/GIF/PNG and Configuring the Compression Rate

Images that have been revised are then imported into Flash. File formats, which can be imported into Flash, are JPG, GIF and PNG. The appropriate file format must be selected depending on the image status in order to obtain the highest image quality at a low file capacity. We will look now at the differences and the advantages/disadvantages of each file format and select the one most appropriate for our needs.

GIF

GIF stands for Graphics Interchange Format. This format is the one most often used on the Web and it is very effective for images with low contrast, such as cartoons or blueprints. However, because GIF only supports less than 8 bits of color, we need to lower the number of colors used (indexing), which has the disadvantage of damaging the image. Therefore, this file format should be used for colors with low contrast and color levels.

JPEG (JPG)

JPEG, which stands for Joint Photographic Experts Group, is a format with a very outstanding compression rate. Users can also directly adjust the compression rate; however, the greater the rate, the greater the damage done to the image. This format is mostly used for inserting images with high contrast (accurate images). In addition, repeatedly saving in JPEG format can damage the image, therefore, it is suggested that the original file be saved.

Before importing into Flash, we want to set the Quality of the image to 10-12 (the least amount of damage). As was mentioned before, we want to import the best quality image into Flash because Flash has its own individual compression feature.

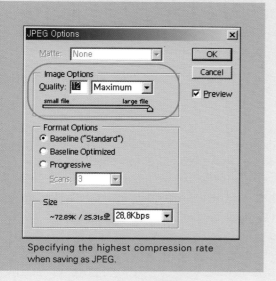

Specifying the highest compression rate when saving as JPEG.

PNG

PNG, Portable Network Graphics, is a new format that has been made to include all the effective features of both JPEG and GIF. In other words, PNG contains both the transparency support and interlacing features of GIF and the level-by-level compression rate selection of JPEG. Although we can use GIF for using transparent images in Flash, PNG would be a better choice. However, because PNG formats are larger in size than other formats, it is recommended that this format only be used for transparent images. (A detailed explanation on making transparent PNG files is given in Chapter 5 "My Own Christmas Card.")

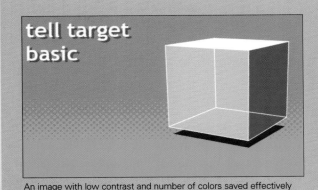

An image with low contrast and number of colors saved effectively as GIF

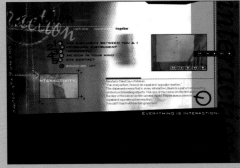

An image with a higher number of colors and levels of contrast saved effectively as JPG

However, as shown in the following illustration, when using transparent files in Flash, it is a good idea to use PNG files, with alpha channels, to clean up the contours of the image before importing it into Flash. Although we can load JPG and GIF files into Flash and then break them apart before cropping the image around the outline, this results in less precision than if we had used PNG.

PNG file loaded into Flash after cutting out the background

Saved as JPG and loaded into Flash

Optimizing Images in Flash

The following shows how we can load bitmap files into Flash.

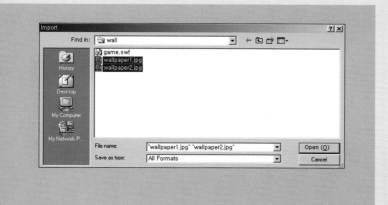

1 ·· Select [File]-[Import] to open the [Import] dialogue box.

2 ·· Selecting all the files you want, press the [Open] button.

The files should now have been imported into Flash. If some files have not been imported into Flash, it means that either the layers on which the images will be placed are locked or there are no frames.

Readjusting the Compression Rate in the Bitmap Properties Dialogue Box

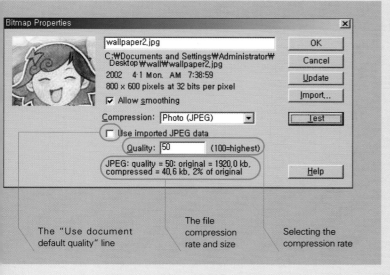

The "Use document default quality" line

The file compression rate and size

Selecting the compression rate

Although we cannot readjust the compression rate for GIF files once they have been imported into Flash, we can readjust the rate for JPG files in the [Bitmap Properties] dialogue box. In this dialogue box, we can specify different compression rates for different files to more effectively manage the file capacity and quality of the images.

In the [Bitmap Properties] dialogue box, we can specify the compression rate and then use the [Test] button to preview the degree of compression when the image is exported. Information on the file, including compression rate and file size, can be found at the bottom of the window. (In order to open the [Bitmap Properties] dialogue box, right-click the mouse on the respective bitmap image in the library and select [Properties] from the menu that appears.)

However, in making a movie, it sometimes happens that we do not get the result we were hoping for. The same goes for using images. Throughout the movie, we will have images that make up a large part of the movie and images that do not. This is why we need to readjust the compression rate of the movie, depending on how it will be used, during this last step.

Importing Video Clips

In addition to the method of using continuous still cuts to express movement, as we did earlier, we can now directly import video format files into Flash MX. Additionally, the imported video clips can be published as SWF or QuickTime file formats. We can also import a greater variety of file formats, if we have greater than QuickTime 4.0 or DirectX 7 installed on our systems, including MOV, AVI, MPG/MPEG.

Video Import Support Format

The following is for systems with greater than QuickTime 4.0.
(Windows/Macintosh)

File Type	Extension	Windows QuickTime Version	Macintosh QuickTime Version
AVI	.avi	4	4
DVD Files	.dv	4	4
MPEG	.mpg,mpeg	4	4
QuickTime Movies	.mov	4	4

For systems with greater than DirectX 7.0 (Windows), additional video formats can be imported.

File Type	Extension	Windows QuickTime Version
AVI	.avi	4
MPEG	.mpg, mpeg	4
Windows Media File	.wmv, asf	4

Flash uses a compressed CODEC, called SORENSON SPARK, when importing/exporting videos.

There are two different file compression methods, spatial and temporal. SORENSON SPARK uses the temporal compression method. In the temporal compression method, it remembers the information of nearby frames and replaces identical information and adds new information. Let's use a newscast as an example. There will be little change in the frames of this video clip, therefore, the compression rate will be high. In the same way, in order to obtain a good compression rate in Flash, it is advisable to use a video clip with small changes or with as little noise as possible.

There are instances when the audio within a video is not imported. This is most often seen when importing MPG/MPEG files in QuickTime.

Importing Video Files

Let's now try importing video clips into Flash. There are two different types of import methods: Embedded files and "Linked files". When importing mov files, we use the "Linked files" option. For other file formats, it is quicker to use the [Import Video Settings] dialogue box rather than going through the Import Video window.

[**Importing Video Clips as Embedded Files**] . . . . .

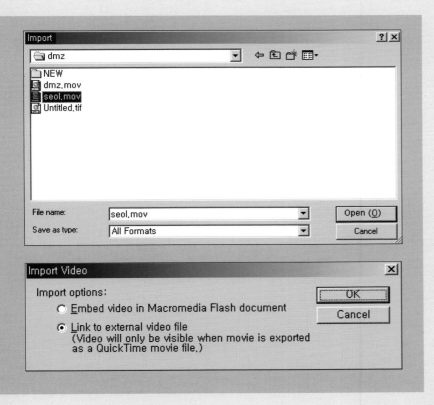

1 ·· Select [File]-[Import] to open the seol.mov file from the supplementary CD-ROM.

2 ·· After selecting the file, press the [Open] button to open [Import video].

There are two different ways to import video files. The first method, "Embedded files," involves embedding the file within Flash and the second, "Linked files," involves leaving the video where it is and linking to it instead. In the first method, the imported video clip file will be made into a symbol within Flash and treated with several symbol effects. The advantage of this method is that the file can be re-edited in Flash and can be run without error in any system running Flash. The second method, "Linked files," files can only be exported as mov files, unlike the "Embedded files" option, and links are made from Flash to an external video clip. Video files imported into Flash using the "Linked files" option are saved in the library as video clips and are controlled through Flash.

3 Selecting "Embed video in macromedia flash document" imports the file.

4 This should open the [Impost video settings] window. In this window, we can establish the settings for the Quality, Keyframe interval and scale.

5 The last step in the import process occurs when the current Flash timeline does not fit the timeline of the imported movie. A window will appear asking us whether we wish to expand it to fit the size of the movie. When we press the button without establishing the size of the movie, the frames will be created automatically to fit the size of the imported movie.

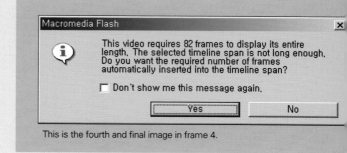

This is the fourth and final image in frame 4.

Import Video Settings Option

Quality

This is where we can establish the compression rate for the movie, which, by extension, affects the quality of the movie. The higher the number the greater the quality.

Keyframe interval

As mentioned before, the spatial compression method remembers previous information and removes unnecessary information. The Keyframe interval allows us to establish just how much of the previous information is remembered. For example, if we set the value to "30," it will only remember data for the previous 30 frames to create the information for the current frame. In other words, setting the value to "1" will have it remember only the data for its own frame so that there are no changes in the data. As a result, the higher the number, the greater the quality, but also the more fine changes there are in the information.

Scale

This allows us to establish the size of the movie. The greater the number, the more the original size is maintained.

Syncronize

The settings for this option allow the movie to be imported in time to the Flash frame rate. For example, if the frame rate in Flash is set to "10" and the frame rate of the movie is set to "30," movie information will be imported into Flash once every 3 frames.

Number of video frames to encode per number of Flash frames

If you want the imported movie to be arranged on the timeline at 1-frame intervals, you would select 1:1 and if you want the movie to be arranged at 2-frame intervals, you would select 1:2. This option allows us to establish how we want to arrange the imported movie on the timeline.

Import audio

This allows us to select whether we want to import the embedded sound at the same time.

6 ** The following shows the frames arranged on the timeline. The video clip will be created and saved in the library as shown.

7 ** Selecting this, press F8 to save it as a movie clip symbol. The video clip, which has been saved as a movie clip symbol, can be given effects and edited in Flash, like other bitmap and vector symbols.

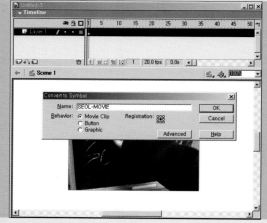

[Importing Video Clips as Linked Files] • • • • •

For QuickTime files, we use the "Linked files" option when importing them into Flash. The imported linked QuickTime movie is not saved within Flash, but Flash only remembers its location to control the movie clip through actions. However, files imported using the "Linked files" option can only be seen when exporting as QuickTime movies.

1 ·· Select [File]-[Import] to open the pup-pet.mov file from the supplementary CD-ROM.

2 ·· Selecting the file, press the [Open] button to reveal the [Import Video] box.

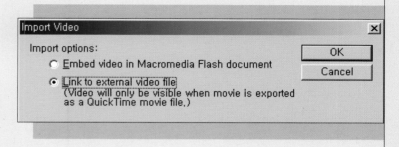

3 ·· Selecting "link to external video file," I open the file.

4 ·· As before, the final step in the import process occurs when the current Flash timeline does not fit the timeline of the imported movie. A window will appear asking us whether we wish to expand it to fit the size of the movie. Pressing the "Yes" button without establishing the size of the movie first will automatically fit the frames to the size of the imported movie.

61

5 ·· The video clip will be created and saved in the library as shown. We can preview the movie in Flash.

6 ·· Select [File]-[Export movie] to export as a QuickTime file (*.mov).

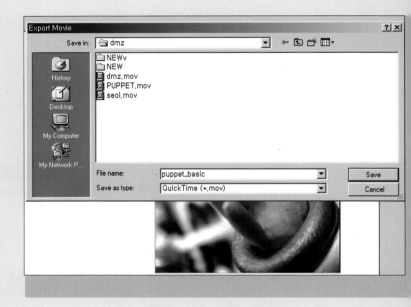

If the directory route for the linked QuickTime movie has changed, use the "Properties" feature in the library to re-establish the settings.

1 ·· Selecting the linked QuickTime movie from the library, select "Properties" from the library Option Menu.

2 ·· Re-establish the directory route in the [Linked Video Properties] window.

Using Video Clips

Because images in Flash are created with the premise that they will be displayed on the Web, many file size restrictions follow. This is why sometimes we cannot display all the cuts that we want to show. Therefore, it is important to use a small amount of image cuts and apply effective change when using them. Let's find out now how these video clips are used in Flash.

Using Looped Images

For continuous cuts, it is more effective to loop together images that flow naturally from start to finish. Blinking of the eyes, lifting of the head, turning 360 degrees and running are all actions, which can be looped. Using looped images allows us to create natural and smooth movements that can be utilized effectively at the same file capacity.

For example, I used the continuous cut of a one-turn revolution for the intro of my second exhibition, which is made up of an image containing a total of 6 frames.
However, I arranged the cut, sometimes uniformly, sometimes irregularly, to create the impression of dancing. In this way, many more diverse effects can be created by transforming looped images.

63

Using the Advanced Effect Feature

After saving the video clip as a symbol, apply the "Advanced" feature under the Color option in the Property Inspector. This will give the image a completely new feel. By changing the RGB values and previewing the effects on the stage, we can select the appropriate colors that fit each moment.

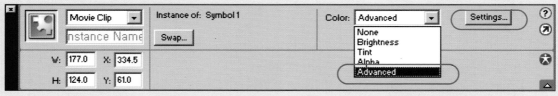

After selecting [Property Inspector] - [Color] - [Advanced], press the "Setting" button to open the [Advanced Effect] window.

View the changes in the rhythms below, which have been made into one symbolized video clip, after establishing the various settings.

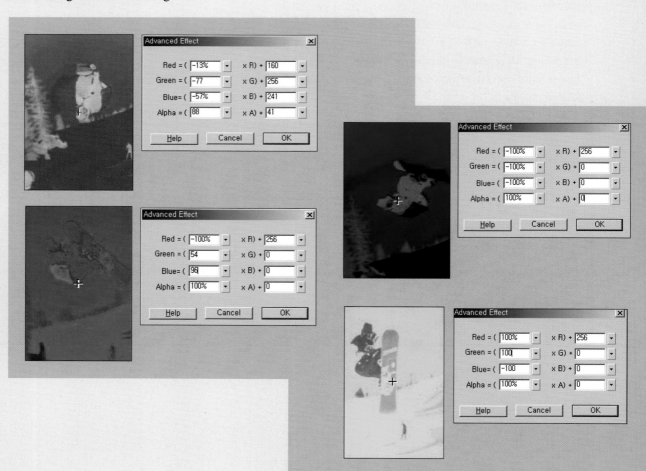

Repeating Images to Create Different Moods

Combining the two methods mentioned previously, we can modify the size and arrangement of the images to create completely different effects using the same image.

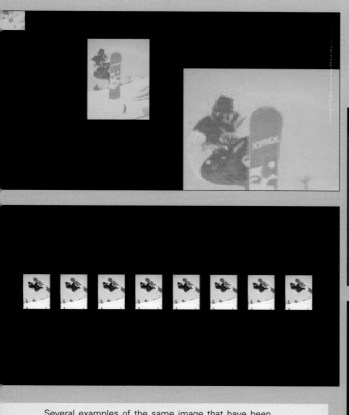

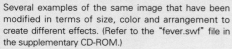

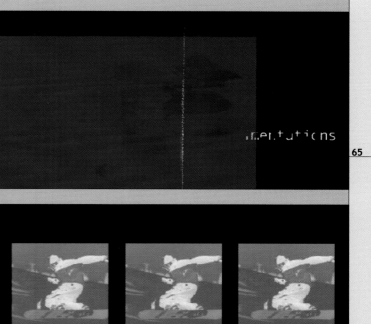

Several examples of the same image that have been modified in terms of size, color and arrangement to create different effects. (Refer to the "fever.swf" file in the supplementary CD-ROM.)

65

hillmancurtis, inc.
making the invisible visible

COMPANY
ABOUT
APPROACH
CLIENTS
CONTACT

WORK
WEB MOTION
SITE DESIGN
BROADCAST
PRINT

NEWS
LATEST
HONORS
APPEARANCES

INSPIRATION
SHARING IT
INTERVIEWS
BOOKSITE
JOIN

HC, INC. NABS TWO WEBAWARDS
NEWS : HONORS

ADOBE STUDIO LAUNCHES
WORK : SITE DESIGN

ADOBE STUDIO FEATURE
NEWS : LATEST

COMMUNICATION ARTS AWARD
NEWS : LATEST

HOW MAGAZINE FEATURE
NEWS : LATEST

ROLLINGSTONE.COM FEATURES
WORK : BROADCAST

ADOBE.COM SITE REDESIGN
WORK : SITE DESIGN

HOTLIST AUTUMN 2001
INSPIRATION : SHARING IT

FLASH WEB DESIGN VS REMIX
NEWS : LATEST

Q4 2001 PRESS RELEASE
PRQ4.PDF

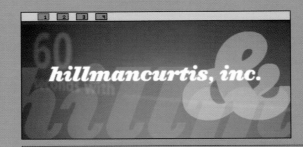

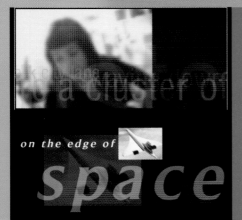

Hillman Curtis

www.hillmancurtis.com

1. What do you think of the "Motion Graphics"?

I love motion graphics. We get to design with time...moving elements with rhythm and pacing, building suspense or fluidity or drama or whimsy. There's no better feeling for me as a designer than to craft a motion spot that transcends literal meaning and communicates deeper than language.

2. Could you tell me what are some features that stand out in your own works involving "Motion Graphics"?

I think I am a thoughtful designer. That means I take special care to identify the theme of my designs before designing. I want every move, every color, every font, every shape to communicate that theme. Also, I believe that every pixel matters...I believe that if you have elements that are even a pixel out of place your viewer will notice, perhaps not on a conscious level but definitely on a sub-conscious one. Finally I believe in respecting your viewer...I believe that the way a site or a motion spot performs is as important as the design itself. In other words, the way a site or a motion spot loads on the Web is as important as what loads. If I have to wait a minute or more for a Flash site to load it really affects my experience in a negative way, no matter how cool the site may be.

3. Please tell me about both advantages and disadvantages of "Flash Motion Graphics"?

Like anything, Flash motion design is wonderful except when used without care.

4. These days, I think another issue in the Web is "Interaction." Feel free to talk about Interaction.

Interaction is so important, and again it comes down to respect. You have to put the audience before of your own desires...finding the simplest solution rather than the coolest.

Flash MX Motion Graphics

03. Sounds in Flash

How do you react during a particularly scary scene in a horror movie? You will still get the full effect of the movie even though you cover up your eyes but listen to the sounds. But, does anyone ever turn down the volume and just watch the mute scenes? Strangely enough, watching the movie without sound seems to alleviate the sense of horror. Clearly, sound acts to amplify (or sometimes alleviate) the tension in a movie and makes the movie come alive.

This is the same in Motion Graphics. Sound inspires the mood of the work and adds life and rhythm to the motions. Two versions of the same movie, one with and one without sound, gives off very different effects. This just goes to show how important a role sound plays. Of course, this is assuming that the appropriate sound has been used. Sound is not just the background music for Flash, but can be used to act reciprocally to buttons or to give rhythmic effects to movies. There's no reason why we should give up the chance to include such a fantastic element. So, then, how can we effectively incorporate sounds into Flash?

Sound Capture

Sound formats which can be used in Flash are WAV, AIF and MP3. Although we can load such encoded files for use in Flash, we sometimes want to digitalize our own voices or the sounds around us. Or, at times, we might want to incorporate a piece of CD music. In such cases, we need to record the sounds on the computer using sound equipment. Although the method of sound capture depends on the type of computer and the generating equipment, I will discuss here the most basic and easiest way to capture sound.

Recording External Sound Using the Windows Recorder.

First of all, in order to record external sound, we need a microphone. Most PCs should have a basic Windows recorder. This program can be used to easily record external sounds. We will now learn how to use this equipment to record our own voices and the sounds around us.

After connecting the microphone (=mic) to the PC, select [Start] - [Program] - [Supporting Programs] - [Entertainment] - [Recorder] to start up the recorder.

After pressing the Record button (●) and recording the sound through the mic, select [File]- [Save As...] to save the sound as a WAV file.

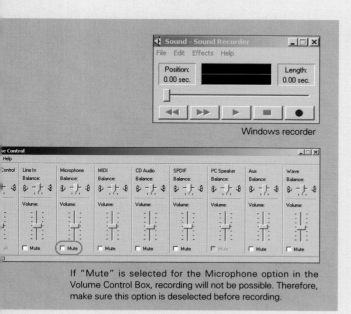

Windows recorder

If "Mute" is selected for the Microphone option in the Volume Control Box, recording will not be possible. Therefore, make sure this option is deselected before recording.

Using Audio-Editing Programs

Audio-editing programs are needed for sound work. PC users use "Sound Forge" and Mac users use "Sound Edit." There are other programs, but we will look at these two programs here.

[
　Capturing Sound Using Sound Forge (PC Users).....
]　. . . . .

1 After opening the program, select [File]-[New] to open a new window. The following box will open in the new window. This is where we specify the recording attributes for the new window, such as sampling rate and bit size and the Channels (Mono or Stereo).

2 The basic configurations are 44.100Hz, 16-bit, Stereo. When obtaining the basic source, we first set the configurations to the best quality and then configure the compression rate later after observing the sound quality.

The new window

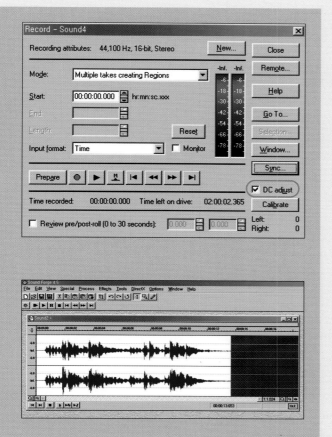

3 ·· When we press the [Record] button, the Record dialogue box will open. The first thing we need to do is observe the level bar on the recording meter. The level value shows how much of the sound will be received during recording. If this value is set too high, you will get a lot of noise and distorted sound and if the value is set too low, the recording will be very low. Also, when recording, it is a good idea to select "DC adjust." This corrects for the voltage between the recording equipment and the sound card.

4 ·· When recording begins, the sound signal will appear in the window.

5 ·· This recorded sound must now be saved in a format that can be imported into Flash. "Sound Forge" allows us to save the sound in many different formats and can also read many different file formats. To change the file type, after reading the sound file, use the [Save As] command to save the file in the desired format. We can change the sound file to any one of the file formats listed under "Save As Type." The default value is the Microsoft WAV (PCM) format. Since importing WAV, AIF and MP3 files is basic to Flash, we will save the file as WAV or AIF.

WAV (*.wav)

This is the standard file type used in Windows programs. This file type can take on many different formats, in addition to standard PCM formats, and we can save this file type by selecting diverse compression methods. Versions following Sound Forge 4.0d allow us to read and save in MP3 format. Although saving or reading in this format requires a long processing time, the final file size is compressed down to 11:1. The advantage here is that, although the compression rate is large, the sound quality does not fall.

AIFF(*.aif)

This is the file type used in Macintosh computers and is the format of choice for transmitting sound files between PCs and Macs on the Internet. This format allows us to not only save sound files, but related summations.

[Capturing Sound Using Sound Edit (Mac Users).....] • • • • •

1 •• First, we need to decide whether we will record the sound using the microphone in the sound control panel or record the internal CD. (We can also use the control belt module on the desktop.)

2 •• After opening the program, open a new window.

3 •• To begin recording, select [Control]-[Record] or press the [Record] button in the [Controls] dialogue box ([Window]-[Controls]). To stop recording, press (Esc) or the [Stop] button in the [Controls] dialogue box.

4 •• Select [File]-[Save] and save the file as "aiff" or "wav." This saved sound file can be used in Flash after undergoing simple revision.

Opening the control panel in Mac and selecting [Enter] -
[Internal] - [External Mic]

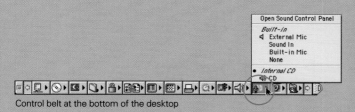

Control belt at the bottom of the desktop

Recording sound

Sound Editing and Correction
(In Sound Forge and Sound Edit)

It is a good idea to go through a simple modification step before saving the recorded sound. In particular, sounds of your voice or the sounds around you recorded through a microphone can have a lot of noise or may have been recorded too loudly or too softly. These instances call for optimizing the sound using an audio-editing program.

Normalize

Normalize is a command used to amplify the volume of a portion selected without clipping. This raises the highest level of the sound recording to the level specified by the user.

The following shows the altered signal of a sound that has been normalized. Depending on the sound, it is important to change the value several times until the optimal status is achieved. After selecting the sound, in "Sound Forge," select [Process]-[Normalize] and in "Sound Edit," select [Effect]-[Normalize] to open the [Normalize] dialogue box.

The following illustration shows the increasing breadth of the sound signal after changing the Normalize value. This means that the volume of the sound has increased.

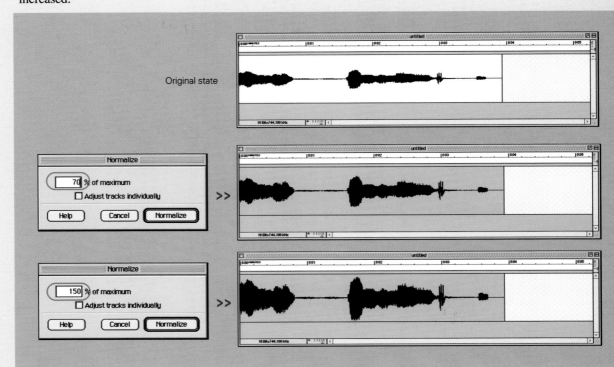

Noise Gate

Noise Gate is a feature which removes the residual noise that lies behind a recorded sound. All sounds below the lowest threshold level are erased. This is especially effective for removing residual noise from the beginning and ending portions of the sound. However, raising this noise gate too high will result in essential portions of the sound being erased. It takes much trial and error to achieve the optimal sound.

After selecting the sound, in "Sound Forge," select [Effect]-[Noise Gate] and in "Sound Edit," select [Effect]-[Noise Gate] to open the [Noise Gate] dialogue box.

The following illustration shows the short sound signals being erased through the changing of the Noise Gate value. This means that this portion will now be silent when the movie plays.

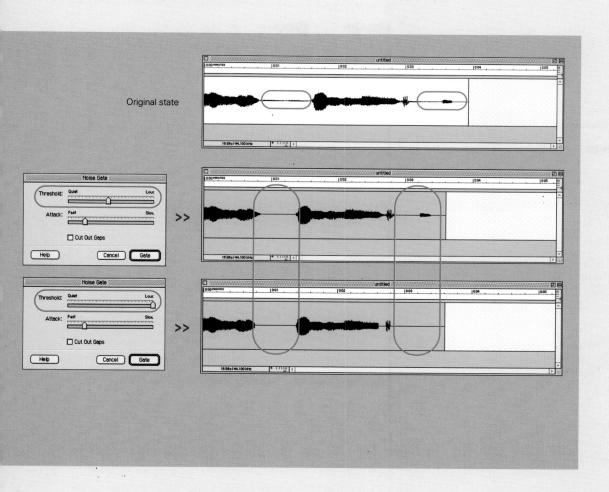

Original state

Important Editing Features for Sound Files and How to Use Them

Let's look into how to conduct simple sound editing, such as cutting, copying and pasting. In most cases, when sound is used in Flash, it is edited to loop naturally. This is needed for sampling a portion of the sound.

• Cut

This feature allows us to cut out un-wanted portions of the file. After highlighting the area you wish to cut out by dragging the mouse over it, select [Edit]-[Cut] (Ctrl + X, ⌘ + X).

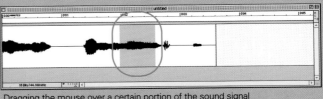

Dragging the mouse over a certain portion of the sound signal

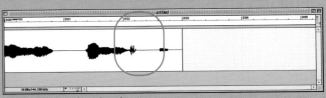

Cutting out the selected portion

78

Dragging the mouse over the desired area in the signal and copying.

• Copy

After dragging the mouse over the desired area, select [Edit]-[Copy] (Ctrl + C, ⌘ + C).

• Paste

The sound files that have been copied or cut can be inserted into the desired location by using the Paste command. After clicking on the desired portion or dragging over a certain area with the mouse, select [Edit]-[Paste] (Ctrl + V, ⌘ + V) to insert the temporarily saved sound file.

For a more detailed look at the wave-lengths, in "Sound Edit," select [View]-[Zoom in/out] and in "Sound Forge," use the Zoom in/out icon on the right side of the window.

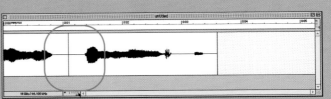

Clicking the mouse on a certain portion of the signal where the copied/cut signal will be pasted

Pasting the sound

• Save

The optimized file is saved in one of three file formats: aif, wav or mp3.

79

tip >>   **Removing Noise from More Complex Sounds**

Let's suppose that a movie with sound is being played on the Web and that there is another movie with sound being played over that one. Obviously, when these two sounds mix, the result will be rather unpleasant. In order to prevent this, the "Stop all sounds" action is given to the first frame of the newly loaded movie. This action is applied to all movies currently being played on the Web and can be used to control the sound of other movies. Then we can insert sound into the second frame of the movie that will be loaded. Double-click on the first frame to open the action window and select [Basic Actions]-[Stop all sounds].

Importing Sounds into Flash

Basic sound files that can be used in Flash are AIFF (AIF), WAV and MP3 files. I sometimes receive questions from users who claim that they get an error message when they try loading MP3 files. This is because most MP3 songs are 4-5 minutes in length and this immense size overloads the computer and prevents successful execution. Therefore, in these instances, only the essential portions must be cut out and edited before using.

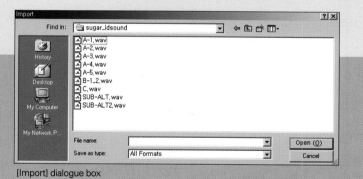

[Import] dialogue box

1 **°°** First, open the Flash Import dialogue box. ([File] - [Import]).

2 **°°** Select the loaded sound.

3 **°°** Clicking the [Open] button will import the selected sound into Flash. We can also import several sounds at the same time.

4 **°°** Verify the sound in the library.

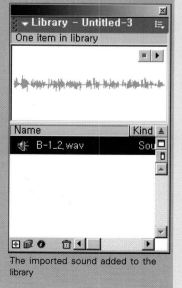

The imported sound added to the library

Readjusting the Compression Rate in the [Sound Properties] Dialogue Box

There are two ways of adjusting the compression rate of the sound of a Flash movie that will be exported. First, in order to apply the same sound compression to the entire sound file, select "Override Sound Settings" in the [Publish Settings] dialogue box. The basic setting is MP3, 16kbs, Mono. In order to change this setting, press the [Set] button and change the values.

The second method is for applying different compression rates to the sound. We do this by double-clicking on the sound icon in the library and changing the values in the [Sound Properties] dialogue box that appears. This method is effective for applying different compression rates based on the character and how frequently the sound is used in the movie. Also, the specified values can be tested right away, allowing us to select values to create a good quality sound of an adequate size. MP3, 16 or 8kbps, Fast, Mono are safe choices. For a cleaner sound, raise the Bit value to 20-24kbps. (The values specified in the [Sound Properties] dialogue box take precedence over the values specified in the [Publish Settings] dialogue box.)

Also, when using actual voice recordings, the Speech Compression option, a new feature of Flash MX, is an effective way to obtain a clean recording of a comparatively low file size.

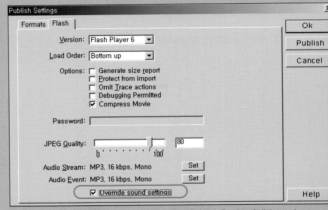

Selecting "Override sound settings" in the [Publish Settings] dialogue box

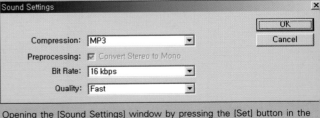

Opening the [Sound Settings] window by pressing the [Set] button in the [Publish Settings] dialogue box

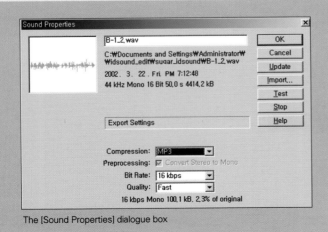

The [Sound Properties] dialogue box

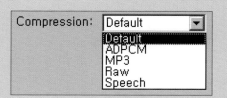

Compression States That Can Be Selected in the [Sound Properties] Dialogue Box

• Default: The default settings apply the values specified in the [File]-[Publish Settings] dialogue box discussed in the first method.

• ADPCM: This is the compression method that was used up until Flash 3. After the addition of the MP3 compression method in Flash 4, this method is rarely used because this method has a lower compression rate than MP3 and creates a larger file size for the same sound quality.

• MP3: This is the most commonly used compression method. The Bit Rate represents the amount of data that is transmitted per unit of time. The lower this bit rate, the higher the compression rate but the lower the sound quality. Bit rates of 8-24kbps are commonly used and each should be tested before selecting based on sound quality and capacity. Selecting the "Convert Stereo to Mono" command will further decrease the size of the sound file.

• Raw: This format applies the sound in its original form when used in Flash. For this reason, this cannot really be considered a compression method. This format is used when a high quality sound, regardless of the size capacity, is needed.

• Speech: A new feature of Flash MX that is effective when applied to voice recordings.

Using Sound Clips

Sounds that are loaded into Flash are automatically added to the library. In this section, we will learn how to arrange imported files on a timeline and about the various sound options of the Property Inspector.

Arranging Sounds

After selecting the frame where the sound will be added, with the mouse, drag it onto the stage of the preview window in the library. (Raising the number of frames allows us to verify the sound signals.)

The following sound signals will appear in the frames where the sounds have been added.

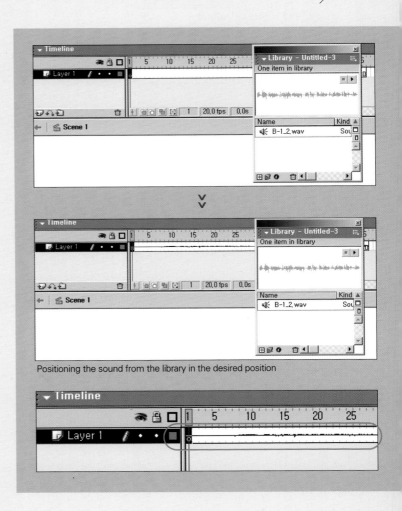

Positioning the sound from the library in the desired position

tip >>

Sounds can also be inserted from the Property Inspector. After selecting the frame where the sound will be inserted, with the mouse, select the desired sound from Sound in the Property Inspector.

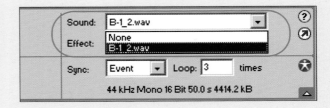

Observing the Sound Option in the Property Inspector

All the sound that is imported into your computer is automatically saved in Flash Library that can be shown on the Property Inspector option. Let me show you the functions of this feature.

Options that are available, with relation to sound, include sound, Effect, Edit, Sync and Loop. (If all of these options do not appear, click on the "Expand/Collapse the Information Area" button on the bottom, right-hand side of the box.)

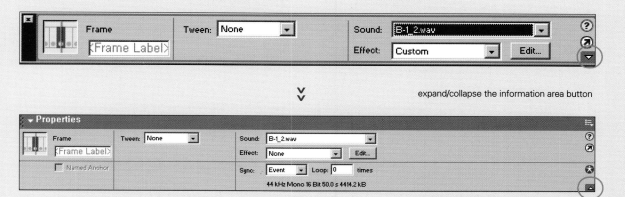

expand/collapse the information area button

83

Sound

This is where all the sounds imported into Flash are saved and it is here that users select the sound of their choice.

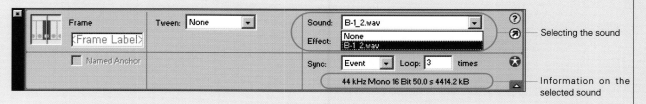

— Selecting the sound

— Information on the selected sound

Edit

The [Edit Envelope] window will appear allowing us to make direct changes to the sound.

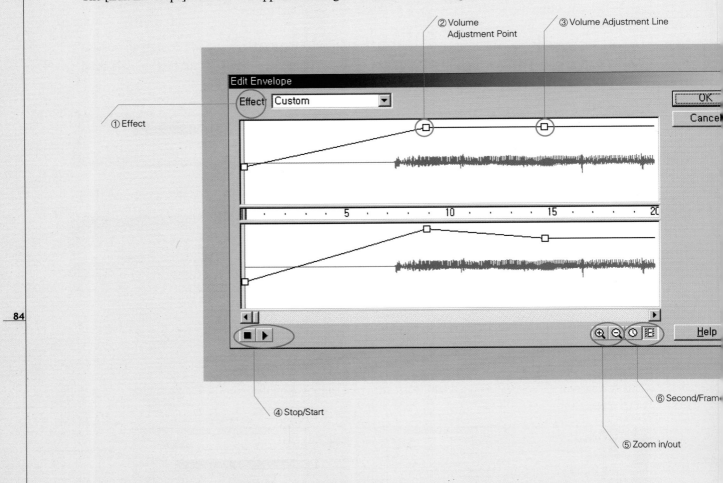

① Effect: Various effects can be applied to the sound.

② Volume Adjustment Point: This is where we can adjust the volume. Clicking on the volume adjustment line will create a new volume adjustment point, which is dragged to adjust the volume. To remove this volume adjustment point, drag it outside the window.

③ Volume Adjustment Line: This is where the volume is adjusted by the volume adjustment point.

④ Stop/Start: Stops/Starts the sound.

⑤ Zoom in/out: Used to zoom in/out of the sound line.

⑥ Second/Frame: This is where we adjust the sound to be shown in units of seconds or frames.

Effect

This is where we can add many different effects to the sound. Selecting "Custom" will open the [Edit Envelope] in which we can add the different effects. In other words, "Custom" does the same thing as the [Edit] button does.

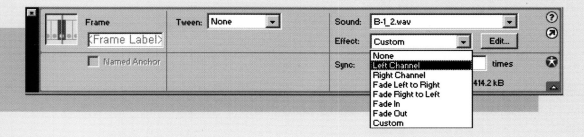

① Left Channel: Plays the sound only from the left channel.

② Right Channel: Plays the sound only from the right channel.

③ Fade Left to Right: Sound fades from left to right.

④ Fade Right to Left: Sound fades from right to left.

⑤ Fade In: Sound gets increasingly louder at the beginning.

⑥ Fade Out: Sound slowly fades at the end.

⑦ Custom: Opens the sound control window in which we can directly edit the sound.

Loops

This option allows us to specify how many times the sound will loop. Because the sound is comparatively larger in size than the movie, most often the syllable that can be looped is sampled before looping.

Looping sound

In order to loop sound, enter the appropriate value for "Loops." To create continuous looping of sound, set the loop value to 9999.

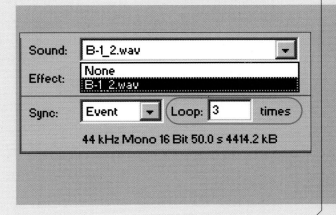

Sync

Short for "synchronization," this feature puts the sound in sync when it is played.

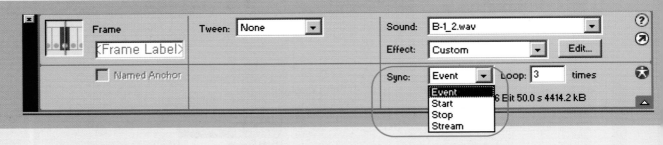

① Event: The sound starts at the same time the event occurs and plays after all the sound data has been transmitted. Independent of the timeline, the sound will continue to play even after the movie is stopped.

② Start: Similar to the "Event" option, but is ignored when the same sound is being played. In contrast, the "Event" option allows the same sounds to be played simultaneously.

③ Stop: Stops the specified sound.

④ Stream: Transmits the minimum amount of data necessary to play. When played, synchronizes the movie on the timeline with the music.

Stopping the Sound That Is Being Played

In order to stop the sound at a particular moment, add a key frame to the area you wish to stop, add the same sound and then set the Sync value to "Stop." This allows us to stop playing when a particular piece of the sound is played.

Synchronizing Sound

In order to synchronize the sound with the movie, select "Stream" in the Sync option. This matches the speed of the movie with the speed of the sound. This option transmits only the minimum amount of data necessary to play and synchronizes the movie on the timeline with the music.

If the computer setting is low and the movie cannot keep up with the sound, it will begin skipping frames to keep up. Also, when the speed is slow and the data cannot be received, the movie and the sound will both stop momentarily until the data is transmitted before playing again.

Bradley Grosh

www.gmunk.com

1. What do you think of the "Motion Graphics"?

Motion Graphics have their ups and downs, just like everything else.... The happy side is that there's a tremendous amount of freedom involved; *ie.*, with what you can do and the various tools you can use to realize your specific solution... Plus, there's never any issues with playback or bandwidth limitations... so that's a big fat bonus point as well...

2. Could you tell me what are some features that stand out in your own works involving "Motion Graphics"?

I find my stuff to be a s***load of cuts, tweaks, electro dancin' and fast fast speedy things everywhere. I guess I'm not into the slow groove. That's probably the most defining quality, I guess.

3. Please tell me about both advantages and disadvantages of "Flash Motion Graphics"?

There's one advantage that I can think of, in that it's made in "real time". You don't have to "render" anything, which makes it pretty easy to animate.. plus, you have a nice set of illustration tools at your disposal, within the application.

4. These days, I think another issue in the Web is "Interaction." Feel free to talk about Interaction.

Interaction is probably the central thing keepin' the internet alive and reasonably healthy. It's super important. It's what has shaped this new medium.

www.gmunk.com

Flash MX Motion Graphics

04. What's Wrong?

We are in here.

Concept

Of all the work that is on display at seoleuna.com, this movie took the least amount of time to make. It took only a day. Of course the bitmap images that were used were pictures that I had taken previously; however, the entire process, from start to finish, took only a day. Considering the fact that it usually takes anywhere from between 3 days to a month to create a movie, this movie was completed in an incredibly short amount of time. I guess you can say that I was filled with an overwhelming urge to create a movie at that time. Filled with desire, I began this movie very randomly. I first wrote the copy and then looked for images that would fit that scenario and sought out the connecting themes between the scenes.

This project deals with the anonymous meetings that take place on the Internet. Without hesitation, I begin to chat.

What's going on?
Anyway, We are in here.
I've never spoken to you.
I've never seen you.
I've never met you.

I don't know who you are.
You, neither.

What's wrong?

We meet numerous people on the Internet.
However, I don't know who they are and they don't know who I am.
This is what I say in response:

"So what's wrong with that? It doesn't matter! At least we're together!!"

Without a doubt, the most important part of this project is the text animation. Not only does the text serve to relay a message, it plays the role of the all-important object. This main object is a very important element that takes control over the flow of the movie.

Text Animation

Texts are the important elements for relaying messages. How text will be used to conduct the flow of the movie and how it will be blended together with the screen need to be considered for all Flash projects.

In this example as well, text is used to add tempo to certain parts of the movie, relay a message and construct the overall flow of the movie. We will talk about how this is done in more detail when we talk about how to utilize the end product.

The important point here is that the text in this movie is not used simply for relaying a message. It, as just one image element, completes the overall atmosphere of the movie through movement.

Text being used in one movie frame

How to Use Objects That Conduct the Overall Flow of the Movie

The circle shown here is the very important motive for linking the project together. In the first part, as the type spreads in irregular fashion towards the outer edges, the circle spreads along with it like waves to help the movement and then moves back to a fixed point to add continuity to the movie. This is then magnified and disappears along the edges and then bounces quickly back to attract the attention of the viewer. Finally, the same form of movement is used to convert the screen.

The Screen Composed of the Circle

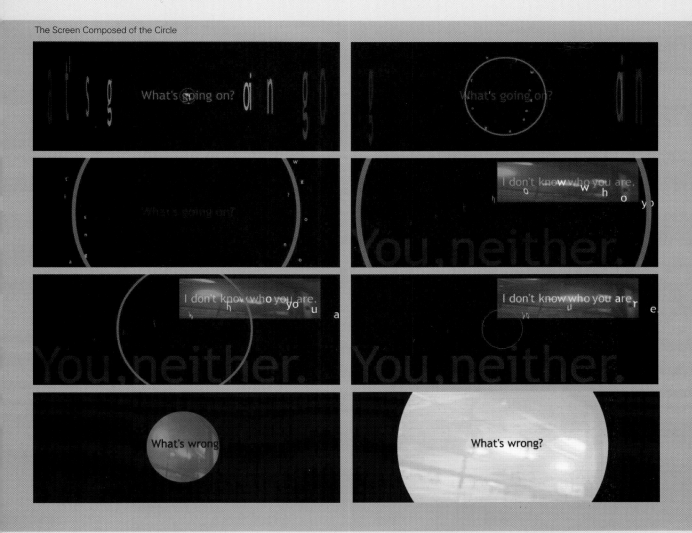

In this way, the circle acts to control the flow of the entire movie. It unifies and adds continuity to the overall movie. Lets's look at another movie that uses this same method.

This movie uses a small, flickering orange box. This box acts to hold the attention of the viewer and add continuity to the movie. In other words, by flickering on the screen it lets the type know where to go or by continuing to move in the same direction it adds continuity to the movie.

The rectangular object that is used continuously throughout the movie

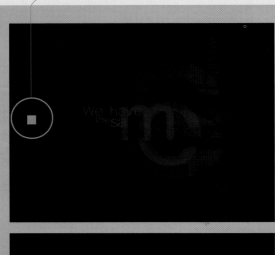

It is very common to use one object, from start to finish, as a supporting measure. This is very good for making the transitions in the movie appear natural, attracting the attention of the viewer and for adding an overall unity to the entire movie.

Using Looped Bitmap Images

The image that will be used here is a picture that was taken of the outside scenery on a moving bus as it entered a tunnel. This image shows signals that are placed at even intervals throughout the tunnel and how they pass quickly by and become more and more distant as the bus moves forward. I chose this image not because it has anything to do with the theme of my movie, but because it became a very important background resource for adding speed to my movie.

Only 4 bitmap image cuts were used for this movie. In terms of time, it was a mere 0.25 seconds of a looped cut. (This movie was filmed on the basis of 16 frames per second.)

The Looped Bitmap Cut Used in the Movie

However, because the beginning and end mesh so well, it was possible to loop this image and use it throughout the entire movie. Using the Advanced Effect feature of the Property Inspector, we can change the color values of the image to create different effects. If you look carefully, you will be able to see how the same image was altered in various ways.

The Modified Bitmap Images

Flash is based on what we can see on the Web. Therefore, it is important to make the maximum use out of an image source, like in this case, to optimize the file size. Using this method, the entire size of this 155-frame movie, including sound, is only 68K. (The sound is 10K.)

Due to problems with the size of the movie and the load on the CPU, movies made using Flash do not always appear as we imagine them. In other words, there are limitations to the effects that we add to our movie. Therefore, it is important to know how to create the maximum results within a limited environment. Using the images as shown here is one solution.

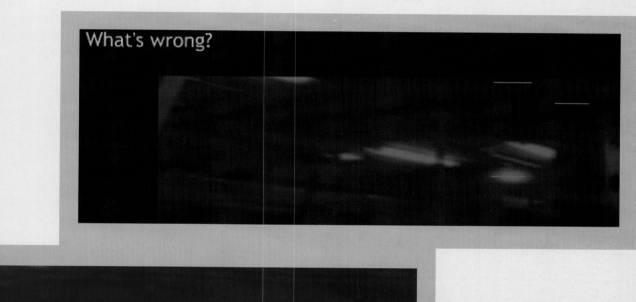

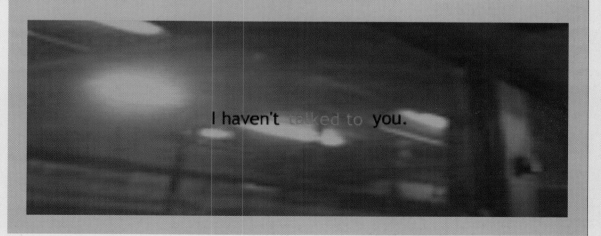

Let's take a more detailed look at the various sources that are used in this movie-in their consecutive arrangement. This movie is made up of text animation and the original animation and motion tuning are used to add appropriate movement.

1) Central Text Animation

In frames 1-23, the words, "What's going on?" appear slowly in the middle of the screen as the transparency and size of the text changes.

In frames 23-40, the text slowly disappears.

1 frame

0

25 frame

100

Changes in the Alpha value

Changes in the width and length of the te

Changes in the text location

"What's going on?" Text Animation

What would be a good way to arrange the text, "What's going on?" on the screen? Staring at the empty screen, I began by first imagining various situations.

"Since it's the beginning of the movie, should I use a fade-in? If that's too simple, should I just have the text radiate out onto the screen? Since the screen is longer than it is wide, I wish I could add some movements that spread to the sides...Hmmm...these movements need to be stronger...."

After much thinking and deliberation, my musings slowly made their way onto the screen.

Actually, in this movie, as the words "What's going on?" appeared on the screen, a total of three other text animations appeared simultaneously. This was to emphasize the introduction of the text in the beginning.

Adding these movements to the timeline we have the following:

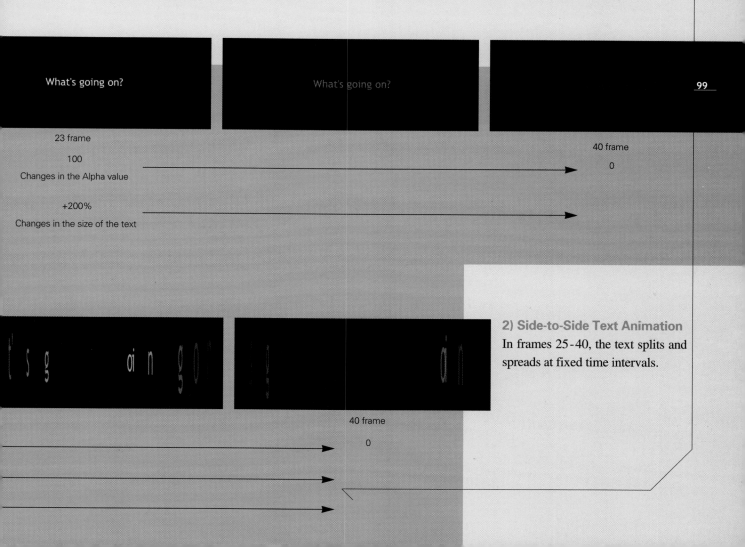

What's going on?

What's going on?

99

23 frame
100
Changes in the Alpha value

40 frame
0

+200%
Changes in the size of the text

40 frame
0

2) Side-to-Side Text Animation
In frames 25-40, the text splits and spreads at fixed time intervals.

3) Radiating Text Animation

In frames 28-33, the words, "What's going on?" are driven towards the center of the screen and then in frames 34-40, they again spread to the outer corners.

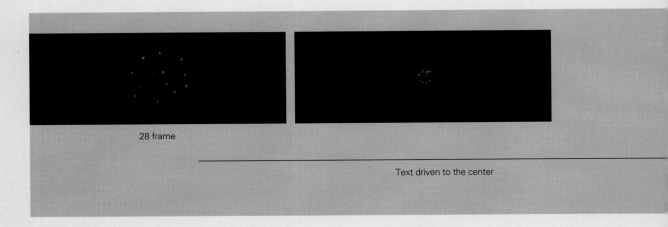

28 frame

Text driven to the center

As we can see in the timeline below, a total of three different text animations overlap and appear on the screen. In addition, we have the circle that aids the movements and, therefore, this portion of the movie is composed of 4 different movements.

Refer to the "What's.fla" file in the supplementary CD-ROM.

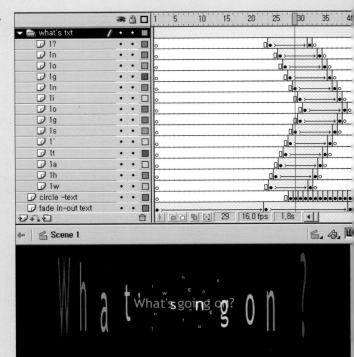

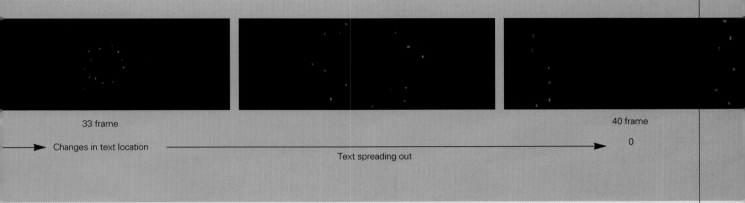

33 frame

40 frame

0

Changes in text location ——————————————————————————————————→

Text spreading out

These are not just individual movements, but are elements that make up the overall rhythm. And, because all of these movements will take place in 2.5 seconds (when set to 16 frames per second), the viewer will only see the overall effect rather than the individual movements.

Now that we know the structure, let's look at briefly what is used for these elements.

Setting the Stage

. . . . .

1 ·· After making a new movie file, open the [Movie
Properties] dialogue box. (Ctrl + J , ⌘ + J)

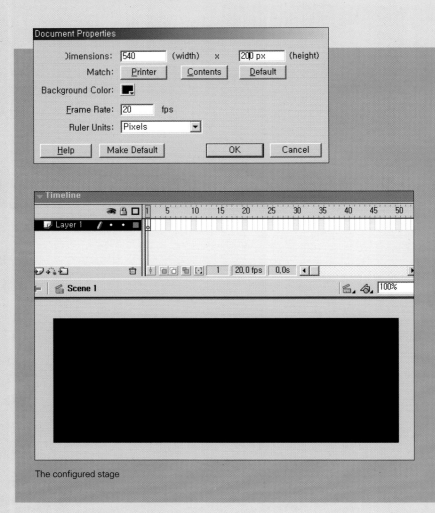

The configured stage

[**Central Text Animation**] • • • • •

Let's configure the central text movement.

In frames 1-23, the words, "What's going on?" appear slowly in the middle of the screen, and in frames 23-40, transparency is added to make the text slowly fade away.

1 •• Enter "What's going on?" using the Text Tool.

2 •• Convert the entered text into a symbol ([Insert]-[Convert to Symbol], F8).

We convert the text to a symbol because changes, such as opacity and tint, can only be made to symbols. Because an alpha value will be applied to have the text gradually appear and disappear, we must convert it into a symbol.

3 •• We can see the symbolized text in the library.

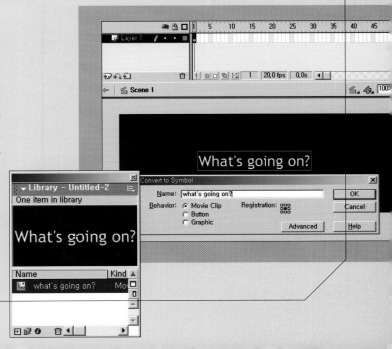

4 This is the layout of the text symbol for frame 1. Since motion tweening will be applied between frames 1 through 23, add a keyframe to frame 23.

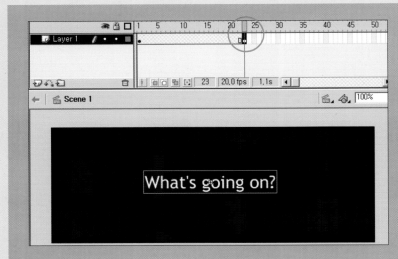

Keyframe added to frame 23.

5 We will now make the symbol in frame 1 get increasingly larger and sharper as it moves towards frame 23. After selecting the symbol in frame 1, use the Free Transform Tool to reduce the size and set the alpha value to "0" in the Property Inspector ([Window] - [Properties]).

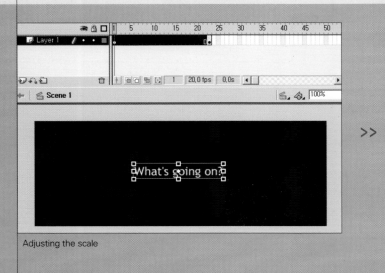

Adjusting the scale

>>

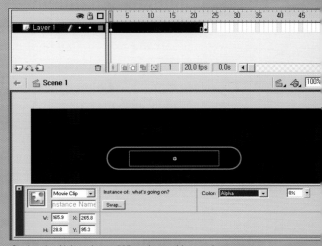

Setting the Alpha value to "0" so that nothing can be seen.

6 Selecting any frame between frames 1-23, specify motion tweening in the Tween option of the Property Inspector.

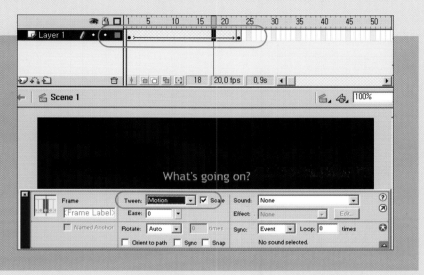

7 We are going to make a slowly disappearing action for frames 23-40. We will use the same method we used above. Currently, the text alpha value for frame 23 is set to "100," making it opaque. Therefore, after making a keyframe in frame 40, we set the alpha value to "0" and apply motion tweening between frames 23-40.

8 One layer is now complete. (Name this layer "fade in-out" text.)

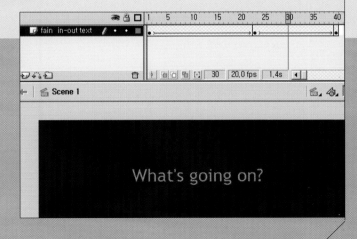

Side-to-Side Text Animation] • • • • •

In frames 25-40, the text splits and spreads at fixed time intervals.

This text movement is used to aid visual flow and we see that each text moves in the same way at fixed time intervals.

1 ⁰⁰ Add a new layer.

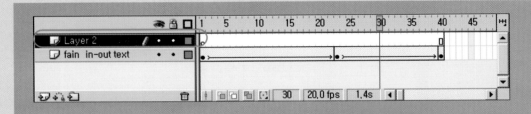

2 ⁰⁰ After adding a keyframe in frame 25, lay out the "What's going on?" symbol in the same position.

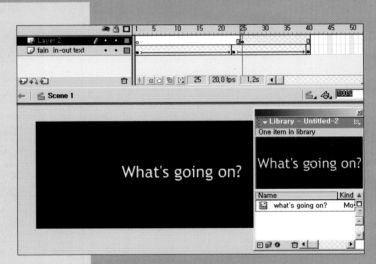

tip >>

In order to copy something in the same position, after copying it (Ctrl + C), use the Paste command (Ctrl + Shift + V) to paste the symbol in place.

3 ·· Select [Modify]-[Break apart] and use the Break
Apart command to undo the symbol property.
Applying the command twice will remove the text
in order as shown here.

4 ·· After selecting the text one at a time
convert each letter into a movie clip
symbol.

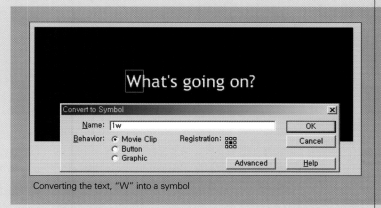

Converting the text, "W" into a symbol

When all of the letters have been
symbolized, it should appear as seen
below.

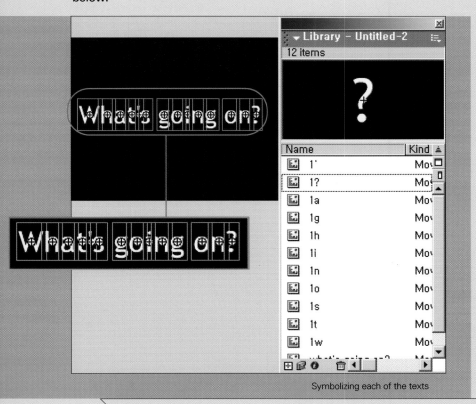

Symbolizing each of the texts

5 Now, disperse each of the symbolized text to its respective layer. It is a good idea to arrange one text symbol per layer because we will be applying simultaneous tuning effects. In other words, we break up the layers because it is not possible to apply several tuning effects at the same time to one layer.

6 Up until Flash 5, in order to disperse each object into the layers, we had to first add a layer and then copy and paste each object. However, in Flash MX, this can be done automatically using the Distribute to Layers feature. Selecting all the symbols that you wish to distribute, select [Modify]-[Distribute to Layers]. We can see that this automatically distributes the layer text according to the symbol name. (This feature comes in very handy when working with text animation and is, therefore, good to know.)

7 The actual animation will begin in frame 25, therefore, we will move the keyframe to frame 25. (Using the mouse to select the keyframe, drag it to frame 25.)

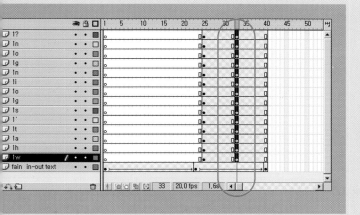

8 In order to configure motion tuning, we need first and subsequent keyframes. Therefore, we a keyframe in frame 33. After dragging the mouse over frame 33 to select it in its entirety, press the F6 function key to make the keyframe. (Delete unnecessary layers.)

9 The symbol in frame 33 must specify the final movement. Because we want the text to split apart and disappear off to the sides, we need to split the text "What's going on?" in half. It is convenient at this time to lock the unnecessary layers.

tip >>

In order to activate only the desired layer and hide all the other layers, use Alt +on the respective layers. In order to activate all the layers, use Ctrl +.

10 Select the letters "W", "h", "a", "t", " ' ", "s", "g", " on the right-hand side of the dispersed text and align them in the same position using the [Align] panel.

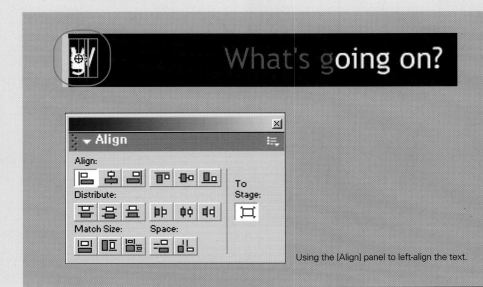

Using the [Align] panel to left-align the text.

11 Use the Free Transform Tool to increase the size and
reduce the width.

We increase the size of the text because the text will
start out small and get bigger as it moves out to the
sides from the middle, thus adding spatiality to the
movie. We reduce the width at the same time so as
not to disturb the movement of the text, "What's
going on?" While the space is reduced, the text will
follow the surface of the big circle and disappear off to
the sides.

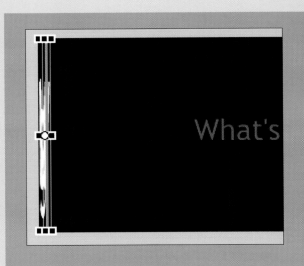

12 Select frame 33 and set the Alpha value to "0."

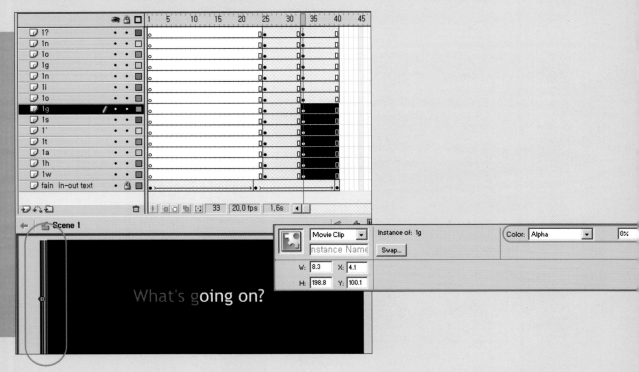

13 Repeat this process for the text
that will be moved to the left.

14 Apply motion tween to frames 25-33. Then, in order to signify the end of the movement, insert an empty keyframe into frame 34.

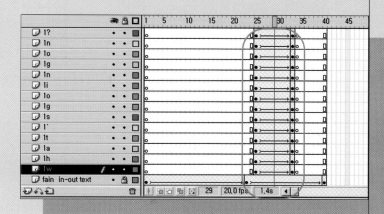

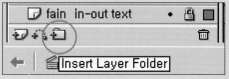

15 Now, arrange each of the layers at a fixed time interval. Because the text on the left and the right need to move at the same time, we make a timeline that looks like this: In the respective layer, select the frame that will be moved and drag it to the desired location or use the F5 key to add a frame. Arrange them at slightly different time intervals.

111

16 Play the movie by pressing the (Enter) key. We can see that the text spreads out towards the sides as it becomes narrower.

17 Finally, we will make a layer folder to organize all the layers. Create the layer folder by clicking on the layer folder icon on the timeline, and then drag all the respective layers into this folder.

Layer Folder icon

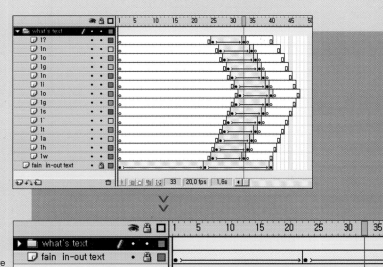

Organizing the layers using the Folder feature

Radiating Text Movement

. . . . .

Frames 28-33: The movie clip texts are driven towards the center of the screen.
Frames 34-40: They again spread to the outer corners.

I named this kind of movement "Radiating Text Movement" because each movement is different and progresses in different directions although there is a fixed pattern. This motion was introduced briefly earlier, but let's take a look at it again here.

There are many different kinds of ways for making this kind of movement. We can, as we saw above for the side-to-side text movement, make one layer for each text and motion-tune it. However, because the motions here are more irregular, we will use frame-by-frame animation instead. Frame-by-frame animation, as the name states, means to add movements to each frame individually.

Here we have a total of 6 frames between frames 28-33. Whereas the text is spread out in circular fashion in frame 28, in frame 33, they are all gathered together. The frames in between create the central movements.

1 ·· After adding a layer (Circle-text), drag the "W, h, a, t, ', s, g, o, i, n, g, o, n, ?" text frame from the library and arrange it onto frame 28. Use the Scale Tool to adjust the size accordingly.

2 ·· Use the mouse to arrange the text naturally in circular fashion.

Arranging the text in circular fashion in the newly created layer.

3 ·· Make a keyframe in frame 29 and adjust the symbol so that they make up a smaller circle.

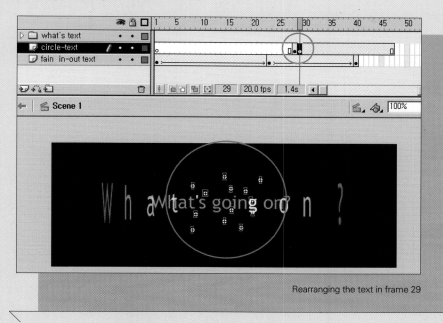

Rearranging the text in frame 29

4 ·· Make increasingly smaller circular arrangements in frames 30, 31, 32 and 33.

5 ·· Make increasingly bigger circular arrangements for frames 34 to 40.

6 ·· Make an empty keyframe in frame 41 to wrap up this animation.

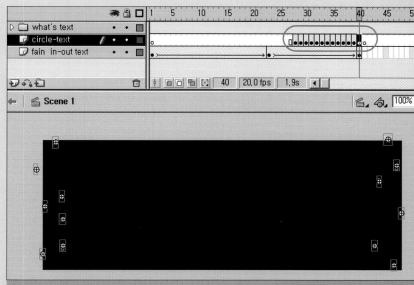

Frame-by-frame text animation used for frames 28 to 40.

7 Press the [Enter] key to play the animation and adjust the
areas that appear unnatural while viewing the movie.

Playing the overall text animation

The Unfolding of the Screen That Uses the Circular Object

We will use a circular object, the ring, to assist the text animation that we made above. This object, which is used throughout the movie, determines the flow and rhythm of the entire movie.

[**Aiding the Flow of the Text Animation**] • • • • •

1 Convert the ring into a symbol ([Insert] - [Symbol]) after selecting the Circular Tool to make the ring shown here.

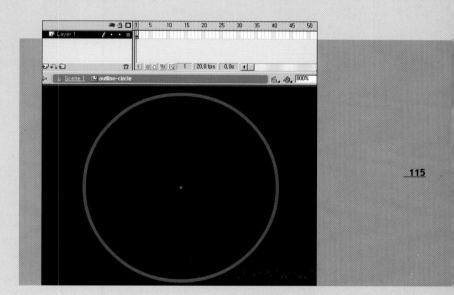

115

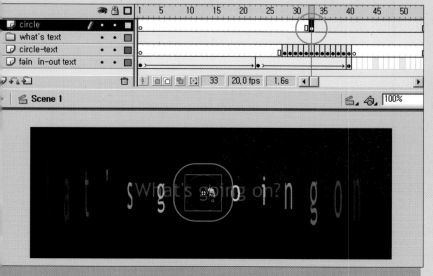

2 After converting to the Movie Edit Mode (Ctrl + E), make a new layer and call it "circle."

3 In frames 33-40, where the text animation begins to spread throughout the entire screen, we will now add movement using the Round Ring symbol. After adding a keyframe in frame 33, drag the "ring" symbol from the library and position it on the stage.

Positioning the "ring" symbol in place in frame 33

4 Make a keyframe in frame 40, where the text animation ends, and increase the scale of the "ring" symbol.

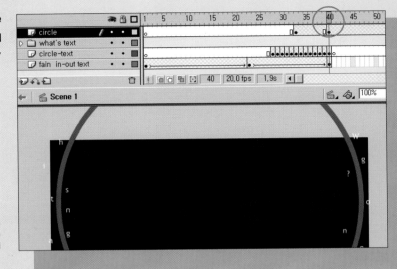

Making a keyframe in frame 40 and increasing the scale of the symbol

5 Set the Easing value to "-80" for frames 33-40 and apply motion tweening between them.

6 Make an empty keyframe in frame 41 to complete this animation. (This is done by selecting frame 41 and pressing the F7 function key.)

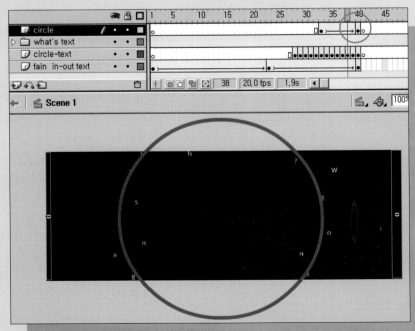

Apply motion tweening to frames 33-40.

[**Adding Flashing Effects**] • • • • •

To emphasize the ring following the motion of the text as it gets larger and spreads outwards, we will add flashing effects. We add flashing effects by doing the following:

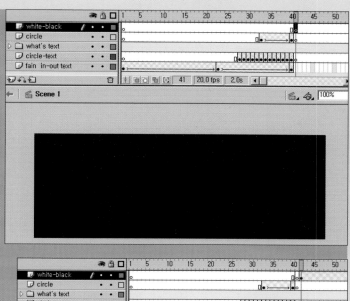

1 ⠂⠂ After making a new layer (white-black), add a keyframe to frame 41. Frame 41 is black and nothing is visible on the stage.

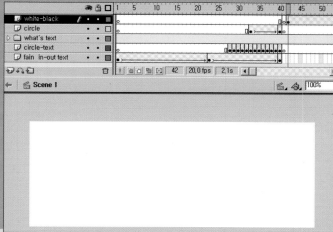

2 ⠂⠂ After adding a keyframe to frame 42, add a white rectangle that completely covers the stage.

3 ⠂⠂ Make an empty "keyframe" F7 in frame 43. This again makes the stage black. In this way, the black and white areas will interchange to create a flashing effect.

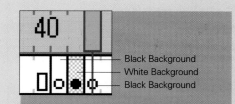

Black Background
White Background
Black Background

If we look at the movements that we have made up until now, we see the following: The text, "What's going on", appears slowly in the center of the screen. As the text bunches up in the middle, it suddenly bounces out towards the edges. At the same time, the circle in the middle of the screen also gets larger and the screen flashes instantaneously. How should the next movements progress? I laid out the following scenes as shown here:

This seemingly has no correlation to the movements we made earlier. However, I wish to use the shape of the circle to make this a continuation of the earlier movements.

Currently, the circle is magnified beyond the dimensions of the screen. Although you won't be able to see anything, we can surmise that this is what happened from the sequence of events up until this point. I want to make this activated circle bounce back into the screen. This will make the scenes move continuously and naturally. I want to insert the natural rhythm of breathing into the movie.

This is simple enough to do. All we have to do is scale down the circle so that it returns to some point in the screen and then motion tweening it. Because this circle is important in holding the viewer's attention, we need to select an adequate point on the screen. For this movie, we will have the circle come back to the point where the "What's wrong" message is.

[**The Movements of the Circle**] • • • • •

1 •• In frame 40, the "circle" layer, the circle is in its activated state. We
will place this, just as it is, in frame 44. We do this by dragging frame
40 while pressing the (Alt) key ((option) key for Mac users) and
dropping it onto frame 44.

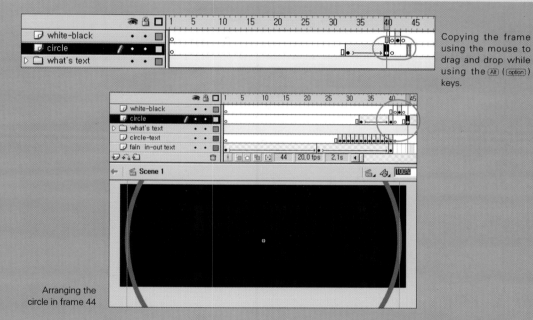

Copying the frame
using the mouse to
drag and drop while
using the (Alt) ((option))
keys.

Arranging the
circle in frame 44

tip >>

In this step in the tutorial, we are
covering only the essential
points. It is desired that you use
the "What's fla" file that was
completed in this chapter to
copy the necessary files and/or
movie clips or to make your own
source files and adapt them.

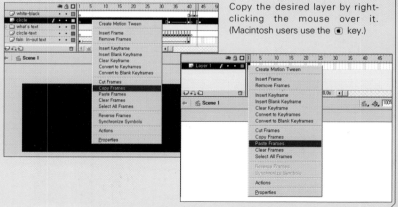

Copy the desired layer by right-
clicking the mouse over it.
(Macintosh users use the ( ) key.)

Paste the copied layer onto
the movie in progress.

2 After making a keyframe in frame 50, lay out the "o" in "What's wrong" in the "circle" symbol. Reduce the size of the circle as shown here.

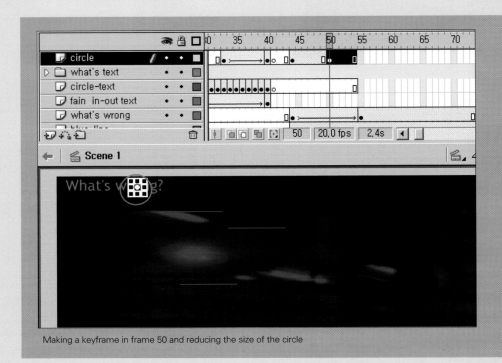

Making a keyframe in frame 50 and reducing the size of the circle

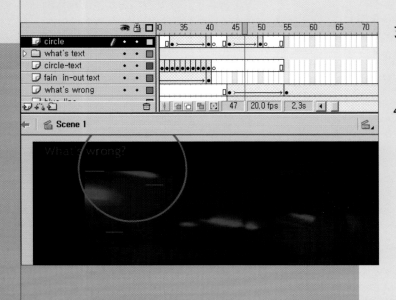

3 Set the Easing value for frames 44-50 to "80" and add an empty keyframe in frame 51. This makes the circle disappear.

4 We have now created the motion of the circle bouncing back into the screen.

The entire movie, from the beginning up until this point, takes a total of 3 seconds. A lot has happened in the blink of an eye! The entire process of the reduction/magnification of the circle has been repeated three times. However, because the point at which the circle is reduced changes every time and because the use of the circle changes every time (i.e. to aid the text animation or to convert the screen), this repetition will not be recognized by viewers.

[Using the Circle to Convert the Screen] • • • • •

In the last portion of this movie, the screen unfolds using a circular mask. In the Mask portion, the process of the magnification of the circle takes place and the masked layer will show the animation that is visible through the mask.

1 °° Add two new layers.

2 °° Double-clicking on the layer icon of the top layer will reveal the layer properties window. From this window, select "Mask." (PC users can also right-click the mouse on the layer icon and Mac users can click on the icon while pressing the ⌃Ctrl key to select "Mask".)

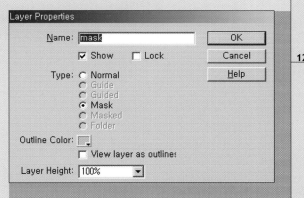

121

3 °° Mask all the layers below in the same way.

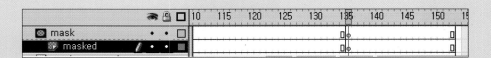

4 After making a keyframe in frame 135 of the "mask" layer, draw a circle as shown below and group it. We will be applying motion tuning to accommodate the changing size of the circle. Since motion tweening can only be applied to groups or symbols, we need to group this circle before applying motion tweening.

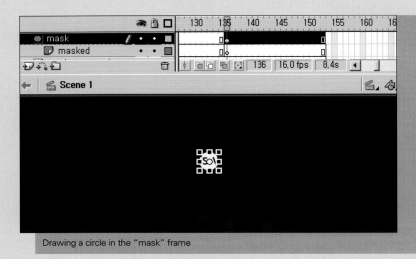

Drawing a circle in the "mask" frame

5 After making a keyframe in frame 145, scale up the size of the circular object.

6 Apply motion tween to frames 136-145.

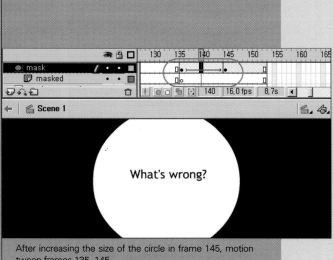

After increasing the size of the circle in frame 145, motion tween frames 135-145

7 By doing this, we have created the animation of a gradually increasing circle in between frames 136 - 145. However, considering that this is the last part of the movie, I wanted to add some powerful effects. Therefore, I made a keyframe in frame 142 to break down the increasing size of the circle and to add a surging rhythm. As a result, the gradual swell of the circle in frames 136 - 142 will speed up suddenly in frames 142-145. In other words, I added some detailed motions.

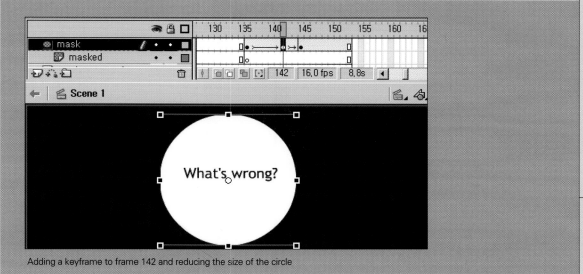

Adding a keyframe to frame 142 and reducing the size of the circle

8 Now all we have to do is to add a bitmap image to the masked frame that will move along with the circle.

9 So that the image in the masked frame will change with the increasing size, an appropriate motion tweening was applied. An empty keyframe is added to frame 146.

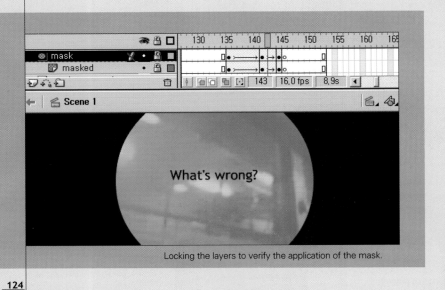

Locking the layers to verify the application of the mask.

10 From frame 146 on, we apply a flashing effect two or three times in order to create a climax after the circle is completely magnified. This effect is the same [White]-[Black]-[White] sequence that we made earlier for the stage background.

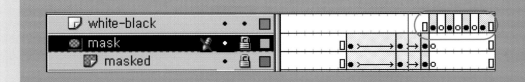

In this way, we have learned how to use the unifying circle to convert the screen.

Using Looped Images

As mentioned before, this movie uses a continuously looped bitmap image. In order to prevent the tediousness that can arise from repeatedly looped images, we made changes to the size and color. Let's take a closer look at the changes that were made.

A total of four image cuts were used to create the looped image. This will then be arranged consecutively in the frames. We used the frame-by-frame animation method of inserting one image per frame.

The images used here are included in the "What's.fla" file library (bitmap folder) and the movie clip that uses the looped images is saved as "redtunnel-motion." Please refer to the contents of this movie clip for better understanding.

The looped bitmap image is modified in Symbol Edit Mode to fit the frame and arranged appropriately.

We use the mask in the Symbol Edit Mode in order to ensure a secure screen frame while the four cuts are running.

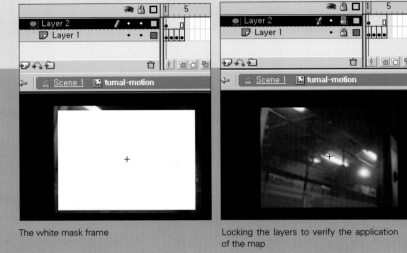

The white mask frame

Locking the layers to verify the application of the map

Now we will convert this symbolized bitmap image into the Movie Edit Mode and arrange it in various ways. For the scene where the words "What's wrong, anyway" appear, after "What's going on?" passes by, the symbolized bitmap image is increased from side to side and the Advanced Effect feature of the Color option in the Property Inspector is set to blue.

After selecting the symbol, selecting the Advanced Effect feature of the Color option from the Property Inspector, make the following adjustments.

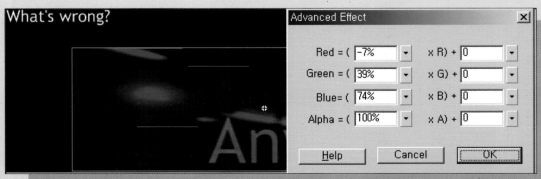

The bitmap image symbol is arranged in Movie Edit Mode and the color is added from the Advanced Effect window.

In the same way, use the Advanced Effect feature and add red or yellow
tones to modify the appearance of the image.

This movie shows how text can be used to both relay a literal message and how it
can communicate visually at the same time. You don't have to understand what
the words mean here. I just wanted to relay the visual message of my cry:

"So what's wrong with that? It doesn't matter! At least we're together!!"

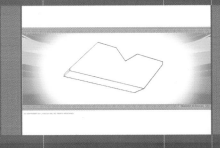

www.2advanced.com

OUR PURPOSE
WHAT WE DO

VULCAN

HOME | SITEMAP

FEATURE

EXPERIENCE MUSIC PROJECT

EMP IS THE 140,000 SQUARE-FOOT
INTERACTIVE MUSIC MUSEUM LOCATED
AT SEATTLE CENTER, FOUNDED BY PAUL
G. ALLEN AND JODY PATTON, AND
DESIGNED BY RENOWNED ARCHITECT
FRANK O. GEHRY. EXPERIENCE MUSIC
PROJECT PROVIDES DYNAMIC.

MORE INFO >>

WELCOME TO VULCAN INC.

Vulcan creates and advances a variety of world-class endeavors
and high impact initiatives that change and improve the way we
live, learn, do business, and experience the world.

PRESS RELEASES

HIGHLIGHTS

SEARCH

ENTER KEYWORD(S):

AUDIO

SEARCH | CAREERS | PRESS | MAP | LINKS | CONTACT

TERMS OF USE // PRIVACY POLICY

© COPYRIGHT 2001 | VULCAN INC. ALL RIGHTS RESERVED.

2ADVANCED STUDIOS
PROGRESSIVE DESIGN TECHNOLOGY

→ 2A.V3_2001 // EXPANSIONS   PROFILE   SERVICES   PORTFOLIO   ACCOLADES   EXPLORATORY   CONTACT

NEW.ME

« 2A.VTHREE.EXPANSIONS
NEW.METHODS.OF.TRANSPORTATION

↓ SCROLL.EXTENDED.CONTENT   AMBIENCE.MUTE +

FEATURE

VULCAN INC.

VIEW

AS A COLLABORATIVE EFFORT
BETWEEN 2ADVANCED AND VULCAN,
WE PROUDLY UNVEIL VULCAN.COM.
SHATTERING TECHNOLOGICAL
BARRIERS, THE VULCAN WEBSITE
IS DYNAMICALLY DRIVEN BY
MACROMEDIA FLASH GENERATOR.

SUB.DATA

NOW AVAILABLE: "EXPANSIONS" VIDEO DEMO REEL

HI-FI // 13 MEG QUICKTIME
LO-FI // 10 MEG QUICKTIME

2ADVANCED // WINAMP SKIN

DOWNLOAD // AUTOINSTALL

UPDATES

11.20.01

2ADVANCED STUDIOS RELEASES THE EXPANSIONS DEMO
REEL, WHICH CAN BE ACCESSED VIA THE "SUBDATA"
SECTION.

11.5.01

PORTFOLIO UPDATE: 2ADVANCED & VULCAN INC.
COLLABORATE TO PRODUCE A DYNAMIC ONLINE

MAILING LIST

ENTER EMAIL ADDRESS:

EMAILADDRESS@DOMAIN.COM   SUBMIT

EQUIPMENT

2ADVANCED APPAREL // DESKTOP OUTFITTINGS

// 2A.T-SHIRT.MODULES
// 2A.DESKTOP.MODULES

TRANSMISSIONS

// VIEW UPDATES ARCHIVE MODULE
// EMPLOYMENT OPPORTUNITIES
// PREVIOUS VERSIONS OF 2ADVANCED

(C) 2001 2ADVANCED STUDIOS // CONDITIONS OF USE // PRIVACY POLICY

HOSTING PARTNER: [XT3E]

Eric Jordan

www.2advanced.com

1. What do you think of "Motion Graphics"?

Motion graphics enable us to give momentum to art. Never before have we been empowered with an artistic tool that allowed us to express with actual movement. It gives depth and dimension to art, brings it into focus, and creates a more intimate environment for interacting with the piece. Motion graphics enhance the artist's capabilities of trapping the viewer and leading them closer to what he/she was truly feeling at the time of the creation.

2. Could you tell me what are some features that stand out in your own works involving "Motion Graphics"?

My works tend to be centered around quick, calculated details that typically don't catch foreground attention, but do tease peripheral vision to look closer at what's being said. A lot of time goes into taking care of the details, but ultimately that satisfies the client. The client is looking for something that is going to stand out from the rest, to show their company in a different light. I try to polish the piece as much as possible, and make sure every element fits the message. People pick up on the amount of effort that goes into any sort of presentation, and so I aim to deliver something that shows a precise and careful handling of the message.

3. Please tell me about both advantages and disadvantages of "Flash Motion Graphics"?

One obvious advantage, as I mentioned before, is the ability of the artist to focus the message through the use of movement, sound, and imagery. It is an infinite canvas. All perception is based on what the senses perceive. Give someone multiple forms of stimuli (which effect more of their senses), and the level of perception is enhanced.

4. These days, I think another issue in the Web is "Interaction." Feel free to talk about Interaction.

Most forms of media in the past were one-dimensional. Input came in, and nothing went out. Interaction involves the ability to receive feedback from the user. We can't talk about "Interaction" in terms of motion graphics because it's only one part of the whole picture. Macromedia Flash gave dimension to motion graphics by introducing cause and effect relationships with graphical elements. The user presses a designated graphic, which represents a button, and something happens as a result. This creates intimacy between the user and the piece. Art is about intimate perception, and any way that we can heighten that sense of perception is the key to expression.

Flash MX Motion Graphics

05. My Own Christmas Card

The Christmas card I made in Flash and sent to my friends around the world

Concept

Have you ever made your own Christmas card and sent it to your friends?

What did you use to make your card? Crayons, colored pencils, construction paper...I chose Flash to make my Christmas card. I made a movie, wrote the words with the mouse, sang a Christmas carol and put them all in a Flash file and used Internet mail to send the card to my friends. My own, one of a kind, unique Christmas card...

It goes without saying that my friends really enjoyed the card I sent them. One friend used the same method to write back to me. How about making your own holiday card this year?

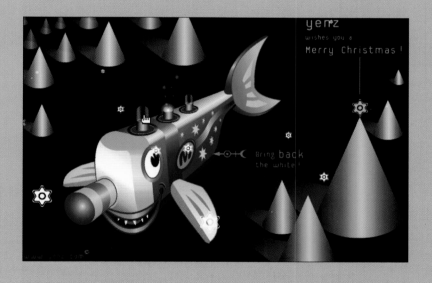

The Christmas card I received in reply from Jens Schmidt, an illustrator and Flash artist from Germany. He used a very cute character in his card.

I aligned several TV screens in this movie. These TV screens were each given their own movement.

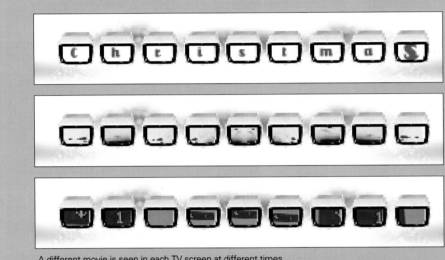

A different movie is seen in each TV screen at different times

134

In order to make the TV screens move, I used the mask feature. The screen of the TV was masked and the movie was set to play on this mask. The animation that was to be inserted into the TV movie was made into a symbol. The layers seen in the movie-editing mode are as follows.

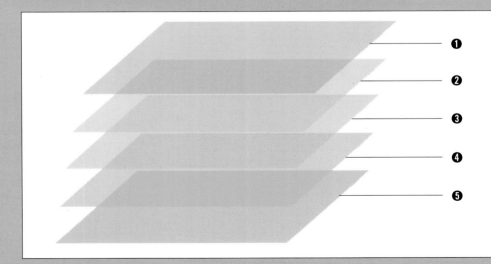

Taking a look at the layers.

❶

The outline of the card

❷

The button, which when pushed by the mouse, will cause the effect of snow falling

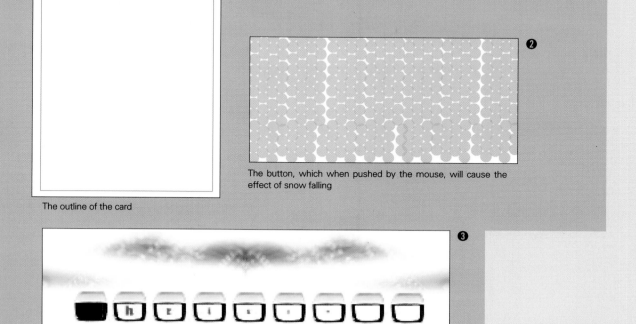

❸

The animation movie inside the TV screens

❹

Hello!

Merry Christmas.

In Korea, It is snowing! ^^*

I am very happy to know you!

Sincerely yours   -your friend-

Text written directly with the mouse

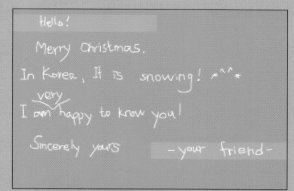

❺

The adorning image

Preparing the Bitmap Image

Many of the images, excluding the object that will be used, include the background. There will be times when you want to use an image without the background or you want to make a certain area of the image transparent. For example, in this movie, the outlines of the TV monitor and the picture tube will be made white. In such cases, the image should be prepared in an image-editing program, like Photoshop, before importing into Flash, because it is quite difficult to achieve an image with a clean outline in Flash.

Loading the bitmap image as it is into Flash

Loading the bitmap image into Flash after making transparent the unnecessary portions

[**Making Transparent Unnecessary Portions of the Bitmap Image**

before Importing into Flash] • • • • •

We will now look at how to make transparent certain portions of the bitmap image. I will use Photoshop in this example.

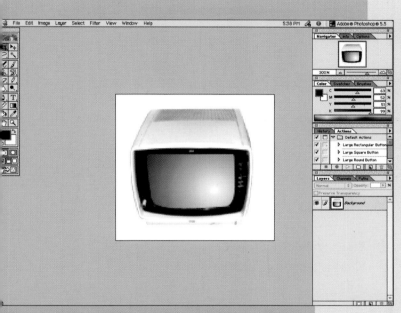

1 ·· First, open the "tv.tif" image in Photoshop.

Using the Pen Tool to outline the white background and the picture tube of the TV image

2 ·· Using the Pen Tool, make a path in the area you wish to make transparent.

3 ·· When the path is complete, select the entire path while holding down the (Shift) key and activate it in the [Paths] palette. (If the palette is not open, select [Window]-[Show Paths] from the menu.)

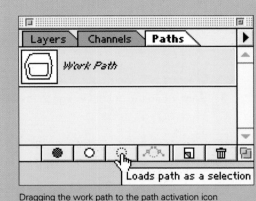

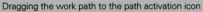

Dragging the work path to the path activation icon

The path is now activated as the selection frame

4 ·· Select [Window]-[Show Channels] to open the [Channels] panel and add an alpha channel.

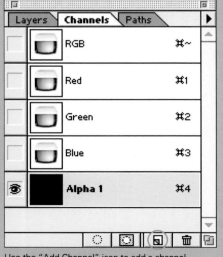

Use the "Add Channel" icon to add a channel.

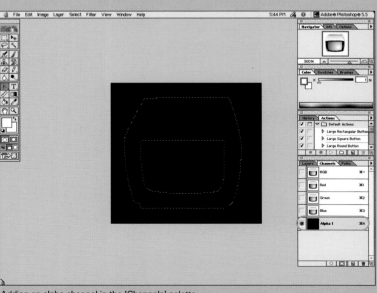

Adding an alpha channel in the [Channels] palette

5 With the Alpha 1 channel selected, make the activated
selection frame white.

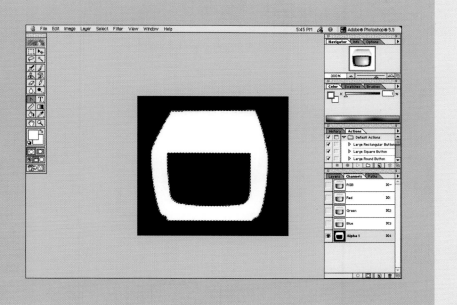

6 Use the Crop Tool to cut out unnecessary portions. (Only what is
inside the TV monitor will appear in Flash. Everything else will be
hidden. However, because these hidden areas will affect the file
size, it is better to cut them out in order to reduce the file size.)

7 Select [File]-[Save a Copy] and set the file format to "png."

8 In order to import this "png" file into Flash, select [File]-[Import].

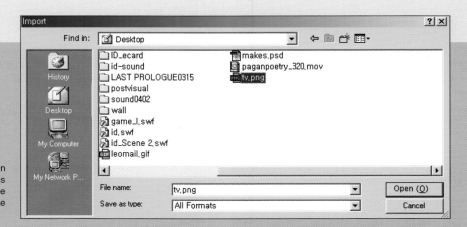

Look for the directory in
which the "png" file has
been saved. Select the
file and then press the
[Import] button.

9 We can see that the only thing that appears in Flash is the white portion of the alpha channel. In order to use images with clean outlines, first modify the image in Photoshop and load it as a *.png file.

tip
∨
∨

Double-clicking on the background layer and converting it into a normal layer.

Making Frames Transparent

In Photoshop, versions 6.0 and above, we no longer have to make a separate channel for frames that will be made transparent. We can just use files saved in PNG or GIF format. In the example above, after selecting the areas we wish to make transparent, excluding the alpha channel step, we press the (Delete) key and save it as a PNG or GIF file. However, if the image is part of the background layer, we must first change it into a normal layer before it can be made transparent by deleting it.

What Is PNG?

PNG, Portable Network Graphics, is a new format that has been made to include all the effective features of both JPEG and GIF. In other words, PNG contains both the transparency support and Interlacing features of GIF and the level-by-level compression rate selection of JPEG. In order to use transparent images in Flash, we can use transparent GIF, but, if we are to consider file size, PNG is a better choice.

GIF and PNG in Flash

PNG files are very effective in Flash. However, for making images with transparent backgrounds, we can either load a JPG and break it apart before cropping it around the outline or load GIF or PNG files with alpha channels. To load transparent GIF in Flash, we need to load GIF with alpha channels, but not only do these have a lower number of colors, the outline is not all that neat. We can get better results by loading PNG file formats, which can support several thousand colors.

Observing the Layer Structure

There are many layers used in this movie, but we will only look at the ones that are used in the TV image and the mask.

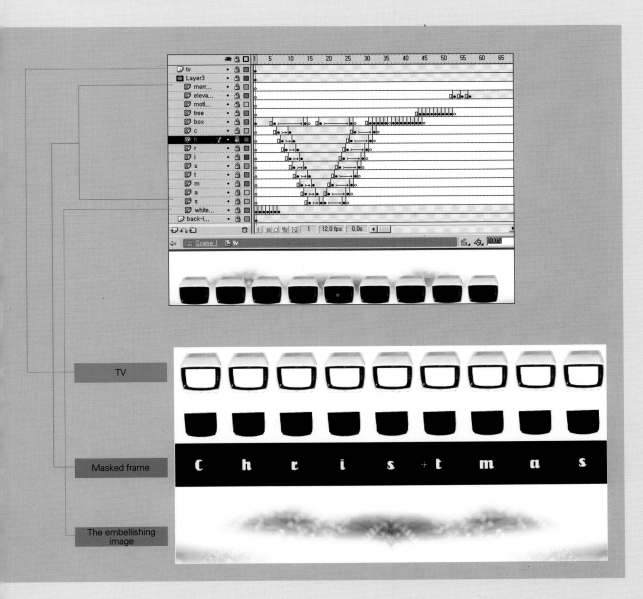

TV

Masked frame

The embellishing image

Making Layers and Adding Objects

We will now make the layer and add the object. In the actual movie, this portion was symbolized so we will work in symbol-editing mode here, too. Of course, this can also be done in movie-editing mode.

1 Make a new symbol. ([Insert]-[New Symbol])

2 Add layers until there are a total of 4 layers.

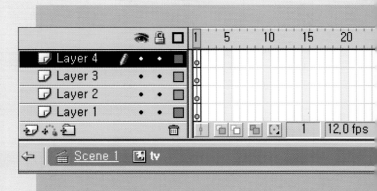

3 Arrange the imported TV image on the topmost layer. Make several copies of this before using it. (Dragging on the image while pressing the [Alt] key will create a "+" sign next to the mouse cursor, which can be used to duplicate the objects.) Duplicate this image until we have a total of 9 TVs.

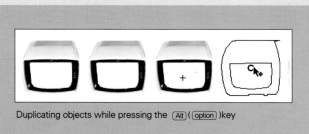

Duplicating objects while pressing the [Alt] ([option])key

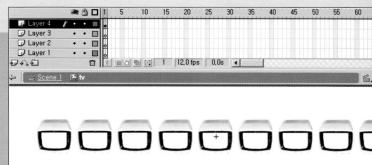

A total of 9 TV images

4 In the bottommost layer, arrange the image that will be
used for decorating the area under the TV screens.

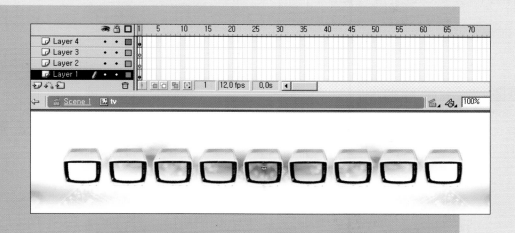

5 Double-click on the layer icon for the second layer from
the top. In the [Properties] dialogue box that appears,
specify "mask." Use the same method to mask the very
next layer. (PC users can simply right-click the mouse
and change the property of the layer from the shortcut
menu that appears.)

6 Change the layer name as shown below and setup a mask frame in the mask layer. Then, use the Drawing Tool from above to draw a mask frame to fit the TV screen.

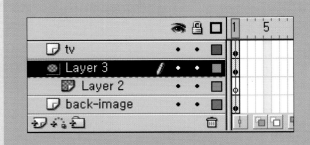

Any color can be used for the object that will be used as the mask.

Important Things to Remember When Applying the Mask

The areas that will be used as the mask frame in the example above must be grouped. However, if another group exists within that group, they must all be broken apart before grouping together one layer. The mask frame will not appear properly when there are several groups.

1. The mask will not appear properly when the mask frame is made up of each grouped object. The mask will only appear on one of these groups.

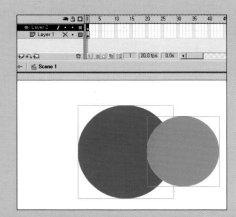

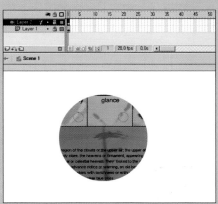

When there are more than two groups specified as masks, the mask will not appear properly and only be applied to one shape.

2. When the mask frame is made up of an object that has been specified only once as a group, the mask will appear properly only if there is disassembled object or one object group, as follows.

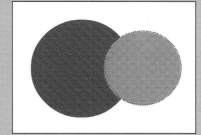

Dispersed object

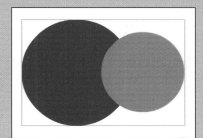

One object

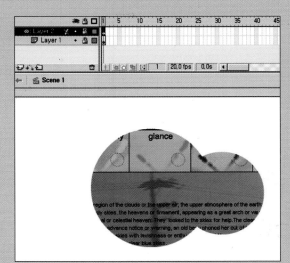

The properly applied mask frame

So far, we have looked at how to set up mask frames. Diverse animations can now be added to this masked frame, as we shall see in the next section.

Diverse Transformations Using Masks

The masked frame is always fixed in this movie. We will now add diverse movements to the masked regions that will be visible in the movie.

I thought about the different elements that went into making this movie. First of all, because this is a Christmas card, I was going to need the words, "Merry Christmas." I also thought that it would be nice to include a Christmas tree. Also, because the TV screens are all lined up, I thought that it would be fun to have them all move consecutively. For example, starting with the TV at the very right, I would have the TVs turn on and off, one right after the other. As soon as I came to this conclusion, I began to work. A portion of the actual process will be illustrated through examples here.

Screen Flickering

When this movie starts out, the screen is flickering. I added this element to create visual excitement. This is done by alternatively arranging black and white objects on the masked frame. This is the same method that was used in Chapter 4 - What's Wrong?

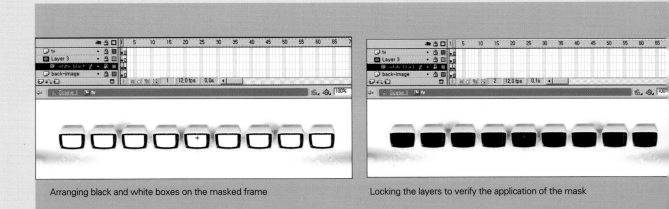

Arranging black and white boxes on the masked frame   Locking the layers to verify the application of the mask

Text Animation

After the screen flickers, the 9 letters of the word "Christmas" zoom out of the 9 TV monitors. In addition, as each letter appears, a black box appears at the same time to maintain the viewer's gaze.

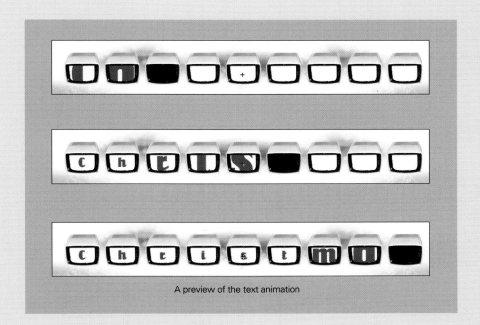

A preview of the text animation

1 •• The text animation here is an adaptation of the method used in Chapter 4 - What's Wrong? First of all, each of the letters of the word "Christmas" are symbolized and arranged in layer 7. Layers that contain movement must be masked so that the movements within the TV screen appear to be moving. If the movements take place outside the screen, it won't fit the concept of this movie.

In order to add a masked layer, first select the masked layer and select the "Add" icon. This will automatically create masked layers without us having to change the property of each layer to "masked."

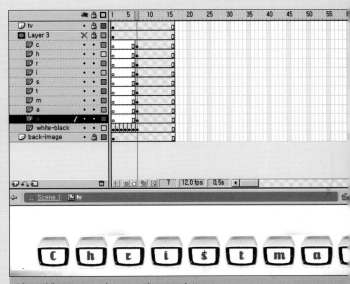

After adding as many layers as there are letters, a keyframe is made in layer 7 and each of the text symbols are arranged on it.

2 Add a keyframe to frame 10.

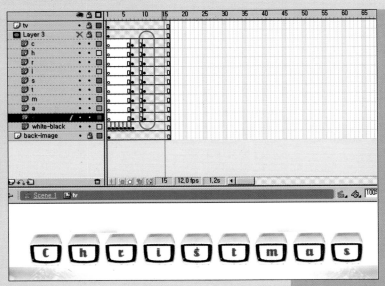

3 Because the text is arranged in "zoom out" form, raise each of the text in frame 7 to 400%.

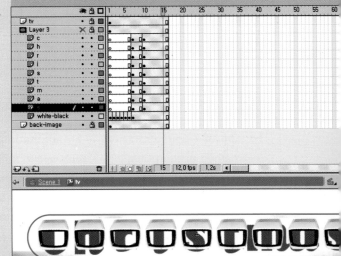

4 Specify motion tweening for frames 7-10.

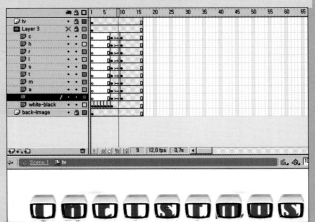

5 To add a time differential between each layer, add empty frames to each frame starting with the masked layer at the top.

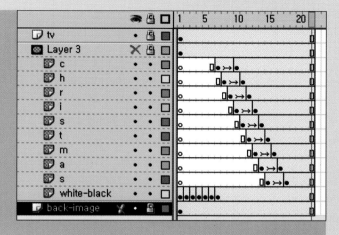

Before the text animation appears, a black box will appear that will grab the viewer's attention. We will now make this black box. Because the screen is primarily bright, this color contrast will be even more effective in affixing the viewer's gaze.

6 Before the animation of the letter "C" begins, add a black box to frame 6. This will place this black box right below the first TV on the stage.

7 Before the last letter, "s," begins to move, add a keyframe to frame 14 and move the black box to below the 9th TV screen.

8 Apply motion tween to frames 6-14, the frames between the layers, where the black box is located (layer 14). The black box should now move across the screen as the letters appear.

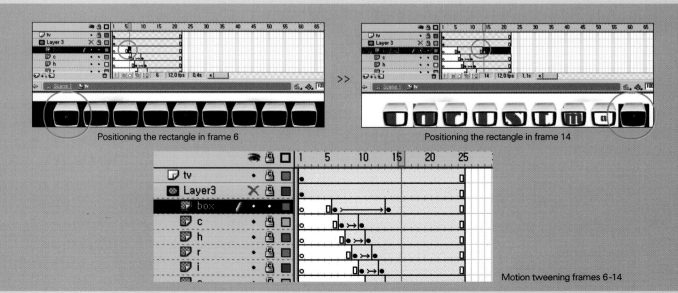

Positioning the rectangle in frame 6

Positioning the rectangle in frame 14

Motion tweening frames 6-14

9 After locking the layer, verify the status of the mask.
We should see a natural link between the monitors.
(The layer was named "box.")

10 Unlock the layer and make the next movement that follows the movement that we just made. The movement that we made now is the appearance of each letter of the word "Christmas" appearing from left to right. We will use the same method to have the letters move from right to left, in tune with the movement of the black box, as they zoom out and fade. As the method is the same, I will refrain from going over this again. The complete layer is shown below. (Lock the layers when finished.)

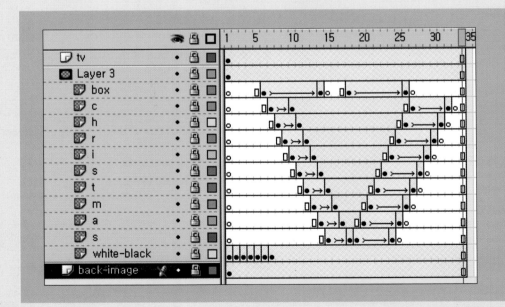

Frame by Frame Animation

There are essentially two methods that are used to create movements using frames in Flash. These methods are tweening and frame by frame animation.

Tweening is the technique whereby alterations are made to the first and last keyframes and the other frames in between are created automatically. This is the most commonly used technique in Flash animation.

Frame by frame animation, in contrast, requires that movement changes be made to each and every frame. For example, let's suppose that we are making an animation of clouds drifting across the screen. In tuning, once we setup the positions for the first and last frames, the other frames in between will set themselves up automatically. However, in frame by frame animation, all the movements in between need to be adjusted by hand.

Both of these techniques have their share of good and bad points and we must choose the technique that best fits the circumstances. For movements with a fixed shape and movement, tweening is the technique to use, and for highly irregular movements, frame by frame animation is the better choice.

The cloud movements have been made here using both techniques. Next, we will look at the Onion Skin feature in Flash used to make changes to frames. (The Onion Skin feature of Flash puts a thin membrane on the frames so that we can see two consecutive frames at the same time to make modifications. This is a very useful feature for creating natural movements.)

151

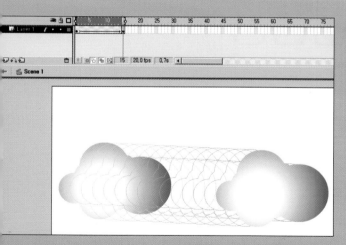

Animation created using tweening - The movements in between the first and last frames are created automatically through a mathematical function.

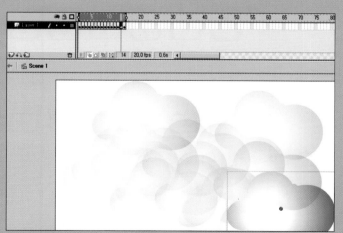

Animation created using frame by frame animation - In this technique, the positions of the clouds are adjusted for each frame, which is useful for portraying irregular movement.

Here, in order to create regular and irregular movements within the 9 monitors, we will use both of the animation techniques described above. We will look at the frame by frame animation technique first. The basic method is very simple. All we need to do is to make a make keyframes as we go along and alter the movements, taking into consideration the movements that come before and after. Let's take a look at an example.

[**Frame by Frame Animation**] . . . . .

In this example, we will create the animation of a Christmas tree that appears from the center of the 9 monitors and slowly disappears. The preview of this animation is as follows:

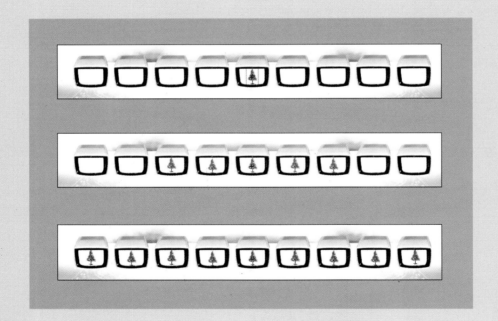

1 ˙˙ Add a masked layer.

2 After making a keyframe in frame 44, arrange the "tree" symbol in the center of the TV.

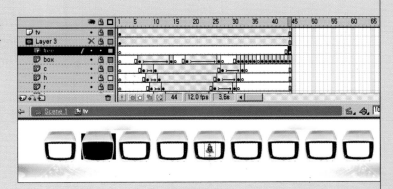

3 After making a keyframe in frame 45, arrange two "tree" symbols, one on each side of the TV in the center.

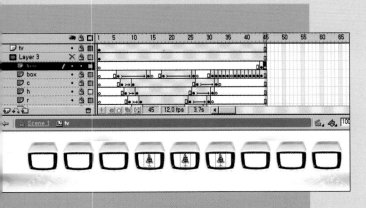

153

4 Make another keyframe in frame 46 and arrange another 2 symbols, one on each side. Continue in this vein for the following frames.

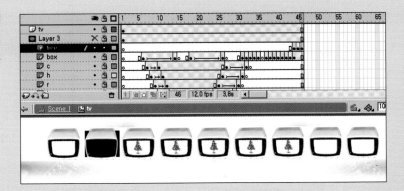

5 In frame 48, all 9 of the TV monitors have a "tree" symbol arranged within them. Now, starting from the next frame, do the opposite and start removing 2 of the "tree" symbols from each side, a frame at a time.

6 After making a keyframe in frame 49, remove the 2 "tree" symbols at the outermost corners. Continuing in this way, when we get to frame 52, only the tree in the very center should remain. Add an empty keyframe to frame 53 [F7] to make the tree disappear completely.

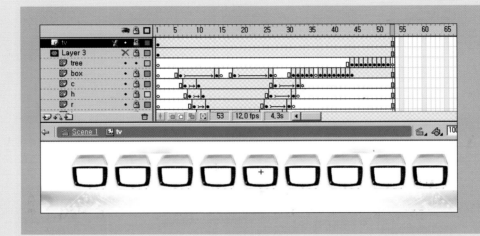

Using this method, we have completed a frame by frame animation that utilizes all 9 of the TV spaces. However, in this example, because we were merely changing the position of the same object, we were able to complete the frame by frame animation rather simply. In reality, however, when using this technique, we would have had to invest much more time and effort by drawing in the objects for each page. Of course this process has its own unique charm.

This movie used both tuning and keyframe animation. These movements were also created in masked layers to make it appear as if the movements were taking place directly in the TVs. In other words, by changing the positions of the objects and arranging the symbols on the masked frame, the viewer feels as if the movie is unfolding directly on the TV screens. We can achieve fun results by using familiar objects (here, the TV) in virtual space.

Now, it's time to embellish the Christmas card by putting together the images (symbolized images and other images) we prepared. Add a layer and form the card as we planned earlier. The structure of the layers and the result after laying out the images are as follows.

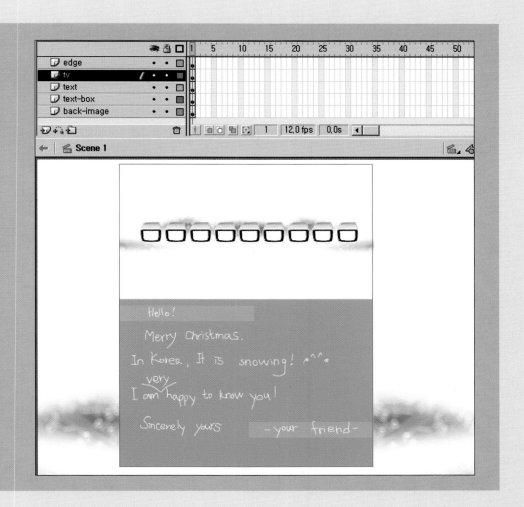

Now it's time to insert the carol into the Christmas card. The carol that will be inserted is one that I sang and recorded myself. In order to record my voice, I used a mic and some other simple equipment. I simply connected a microphone to the computer by using the mic terminal located on the computer itself. These days, there are many headphones with built-in mics so you do not have to purchase a separate microphone.

Recording the Carol Using the Built-In Windows Recorder

1 Connect the mic to the PC. You should have a terminal on your computer where you can connect the mic.

2 Select [Start]-[Program]-[Supporting Programs]-[Entertainment]-[Recorder]. Press the [Record] button to begin recording.

tip

Important Things to Remember When Recording Sound

Select [Start]-[Program]-[Supporting Programs]-[Entertainment]-[Volume Control]. If "Mute" is selected under Mic Options, the sound will not record properly. Therefore, this box must not be checked.

If there is no Mic Option in the [Volume Control] dialogue box, select [Option]-[Properties] from menu and select "Mic" from "Show the following Volume Controls." When "Mic" Option opens, verify that "Mute" is not selected in the [Volume Control] window.

3 When recording is complete, select [File]-[Save As] from the menu and save the file in "wav" format. This "wav" file can now be imported into Flash for use.

Recording the Carol in Macintosh

· · · · ·

1 Connect the mic to the computer.

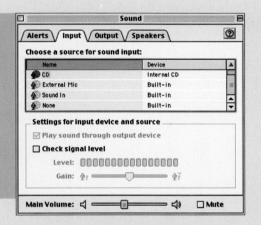

2 After selecting "Input" in the sound control panel, select "CD" from "choose a source for sound Input." Although we can select either "external mic" or "sound input" for "input," when "sound input" is selected, the sound will generate from the built-in speakers at the same time the sound is being recorded to create echo. Therefore, it is better to select "external mic."

157

3 After opening the sound program and pressing the [Record] button, use the mic to begin recording. Although there are many sound programs available for Macs, here, we used "Sound Edit," one of the more commonly used programs. When the program is loaded, a new window will open automatically. To record, press the [Record] button in the [Controls] dialogue box.

Opening the Sound Edit program

[Controls] dialogue box

4 ·· To stop recording, either press the [Esc] key or the
[Stop] button in the [Controls] dialogue box.

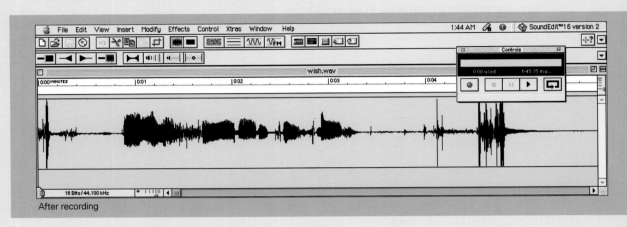

After recording

5 ·· Select [File]-[Save] to save the sound in "aiff" or "wav"
format. The sound saved in this way can now be imported
into Flash for use.

[**Importing Sounds and Using Them in Flash**] · · · · ·

1 ·· Import the recorded sound into Flash.

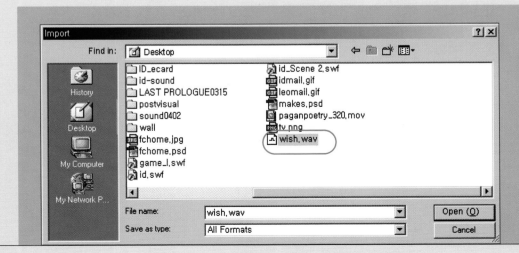

2 Add a layer to which the sound will be added (sound). Although sound can be inserted into any keyframe, it is more convenient to organize all sound by creating a separate sound layer.

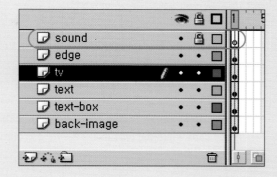

3 Selecting the frame to which we will add the sound, using the mouse, specify the desired sound in the [sound] option of the Property Inspector.

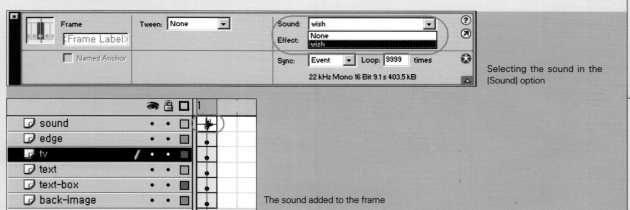

Selecting the sound in the [Sound] option

The sound added to the frame

4 Because we want to loop the sound here, we need to specify a Loop value in the [Sound] panel. It is recommended that a value be selected which will ensure that the sound repeats several times, smoothly and without breaking up.

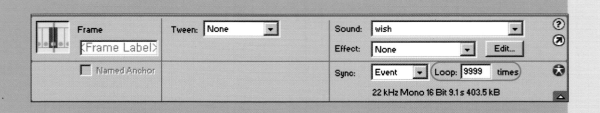

Adding Mouse-Reactive Elements

What is the first thing that comes to your mind when you think of Christmas? Jesus, Santa Claus, Rudolph the Red-Nosed Reindeer...

And, of course, we cannot forget snow. Wouldn't it be wonderful if we could have snow fall down in our Christmas card? That is why I added a feature, which will cause fluffy, white snow to fall down the front of my card when the user drags the mouse onto it.

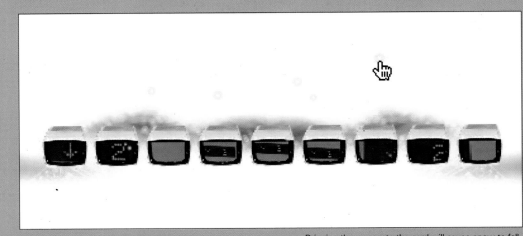

Bringing the mouse to the card will cause snow to fall

Having Snow Fall Wherever the Mouse Goes!

Some users will want to create this effect using a button. They will say that we can add a snow-falling animation movie clip to the Over panel of the mouse. However, that's not enough to create the effect seen here. This is because Button Over animations will remain in the center of the card if the mouse misses the Hit frame and become an Up frame again. That will cause the snow to fall and then stop.

So, how can we create snow that falls and then naturally stops simply by moving the mouse? The answer is to hide a button within the movie clip.

We will look at how to do this by going step-by-step through an example. We will create an animation that starts only when the mouse is brought to the front of the card.

[**Making a New Symbol**] · · · · ·

1 ·· After making a new symbol, name it "snow."

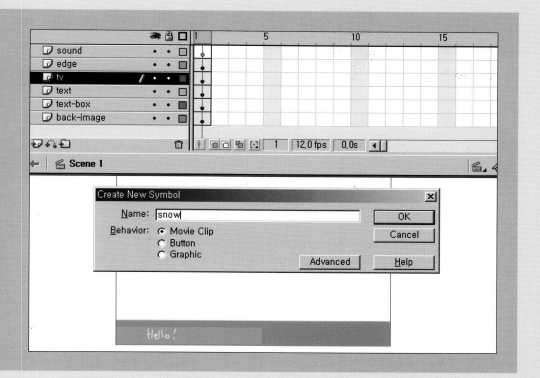

2 °° Move to the symbol-editing mode and use the Drawing Tool to draw the snow. Use the gradation effect to create fluffy snow.

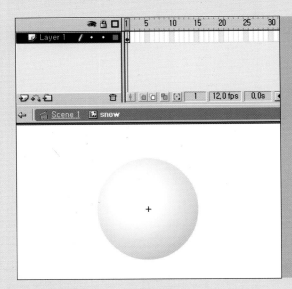

3 °° Make a new movie clip symbol and name it "snowdown."

4 °° Before frame 1, drag the "snow" symbol from the library onto the stage.

5 °° After making a keyframe for frame 20 (F6), in order to create the effect of snow falling down, move the position of the object to the bottom in frame 20 and reduce the size.

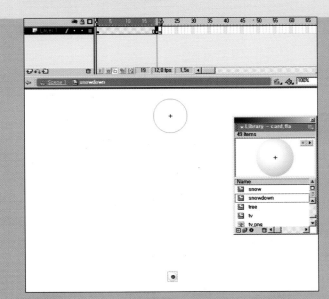

6 ˙˙ Apply motion tween to frames 1-20.

7 ˙˙ In order to have the snow disappear in frame 21, create
a new keyframe (F7).

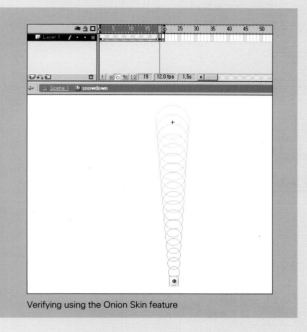

Verifying using the Onion Skin feature

[**Making a Blank Button and Specifying an Action**] · · · · · ·

1 ˙˙ Make a new button symbol and name it "blank button."

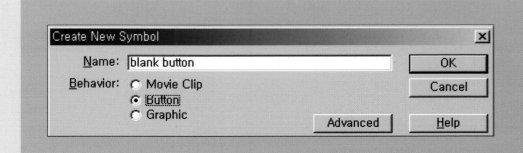

2 ** Leave an empty frame in the Up, Over and Down frames of the
button and use the Circular Tool to draw a circle in the Hit frame.
The reason why we only make a Hit frame is because the only
purpose of this button is to begin the action. By simply specifying
a Hit frame, the frame in which the mouse will react, the action
will commence when the mouse rolls over in this frame.

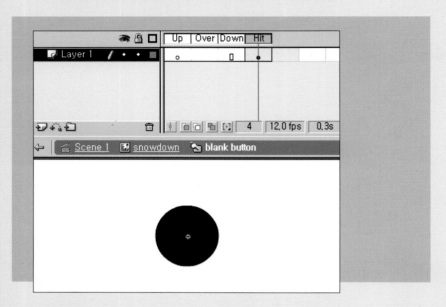

3 ** Double-click on the "snowdown" symbol in the library. After
converting to symbol-edit mode, select frame 1 with the
mouse while there is movement in frames 1-20, and then
drag it to frame 2 to leave frame 1 as an empty keyframe.

Adding an empty keyframe to frame 1

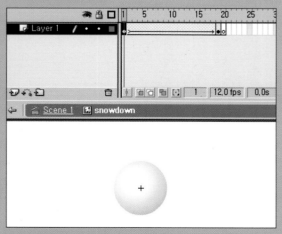

Converting to the symbol-edit mode for the "snowdown" symbol

4 Specify a Stop action for frame 1, which has been configured with an empty frame. (Selecting the frame, right-click the mouse and open the [Action] panel.) In order to have nothing appear in this frame when there is no mouse action, leave frame 1 empty and specify the Stop action.

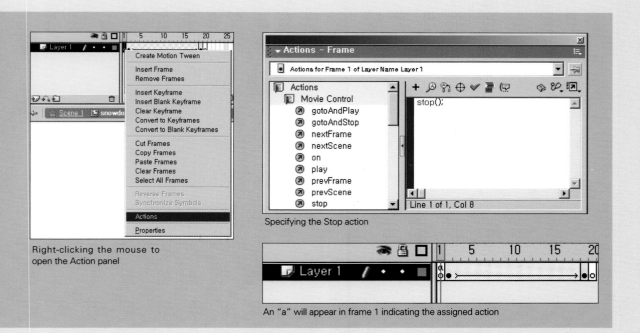

Right-clicking the mouse to open the Action panel

Specifying the Stop action

An "a" will appear in frame 1 indicating the assigned action

5 Situate the "blank button" symbol in frame 1. (This button must be the same size and in the same position as the "snow" symbol in frame 2. This can be done more effectively by using the Onion Skin feature.) Whereas we added an action to the frame earlier, we now want to add action to the button. The frame action plays when the play head passes over the frame and the button action begins when the mouse reacts. Currently, we have a Stop action in frame 1, which reacts to the frame action, and we will now specify the action that will play in frame 2 that responds to the actions of the mouse.

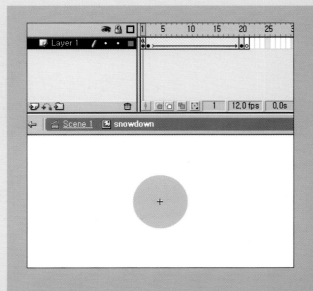

6 After selecting "blank button," open the [Action] panel and add the gotoAndPlay action so that the animation will go to and play frame 2 when we roll over with the mouse.

```
on(release){
gotoAndPlay(2);
}
```

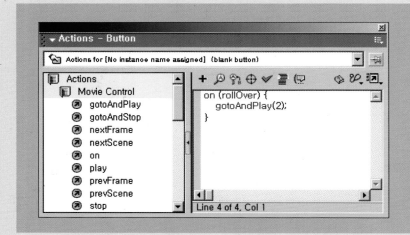

[**Arranging the Movie Clip to Complete the Movie**] · · · · · ·

1 Add a new layer in the movie-edit mode.

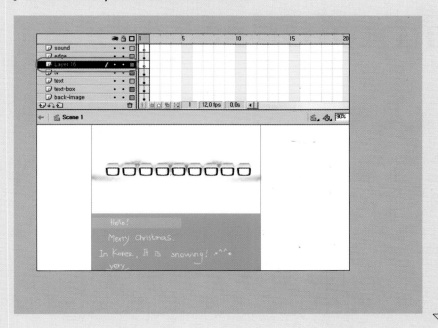

2 Drag the "snowdown" symbol from the library onto the stage. Continue to drag this symbol or make copies of the symbol already in place to fill up the stage with the symbol. Because we have completely filled up the stage, snow will begin to fall anywhere the mouse is placed. (After inserting the symbol and completing the layer, name it "snowdown.")

Filling up the stage with the "snowdown" symbol

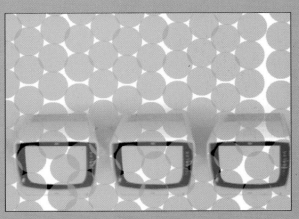

A close-up of the symbol-filled stage

3 °° This completes the setup. Play the movie to test the results.

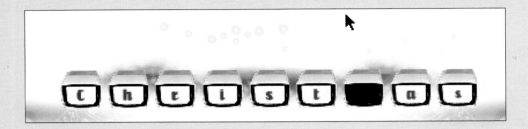

Our Christmas card is now complete.

This type of Christmas card, written in your own hand and containing your voice, will bring a sense of warmth and familiarity to those who receive it. While the movie is playing, the viewer will be able to create the effect of snow falling by simply bringing the mouse cursor to the surface of the card.

Receiving this kind of card will perpetuate the Christmas spirit. How about pouring forth all your effort into creating a one-of-a-kind, unique holiday card for your loved ones this season?

Matt Owens

www.volumeone.com

1. What do you think of "Motion Graphics"?

Motion graphics is a shifting definition. From broadcast to print, to online work, motion is a defining feature of our visual culture.

2. Could you tell me what are some features that stand out in your own works involving "Motion Graphics"?

I think my motion graphics are informed by the space between print and online media. As a traditional graphic designer by training with a strong knowledge of Flash, I think my motion graphics are a reflection of my interest in design beauty combined with the utility of interface.

3. Please tell me about both advantages and disadvantages of "Flash Motion Graphics"?

Flash is limited by bandwidth so you can't really do all the things you can do in traditional motion graphics. What you can do in Flash is create a larger motion graphic experience that has interactivity. In this way, you are giving control to the user in such a way that passive motion graphics cannot.

4. These days, I think another issue in the Web is "Interaction." Feel free to talk about Interaction.

Interactivity is important but it is not everything. The ability to create an engaging experience requires the ability to create something that is meaningful, usable and above all captivating. This requires knowledge of the medium, subject matter and visual language.

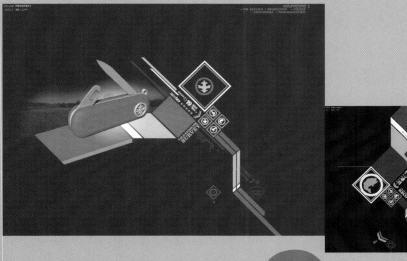

Matt Owens

Flash MX Motion Graphics

06. Episode from the Movie *My Sassy Girl*

Concept

The movie seen in this chapter is one that was used as part of a movie homepage (www.yupgigirl.com). The movie, *My Sassy Girl,* is a romantic comedy with an overall bright and cheerful feel. This light movie was very appealing to me.

My first impressions about this film were sassy, light, youthful and comic. I felt that this was enough to create something very fun and amusing. I felt that users, who were always looking for something new, were not going to come to this site merely for information on the movie and the actors. Not only did this homepage have to inspire viewers to see the movie, I wanted it to be a magnificent playground on the Web.

I included interactive elements throughout this homepage. I wanted users to interact dynamically with this homepage rather than passively receiving information. By incorporating user participation, I was able to complete this project. I invested a lot of time into thinking up the interactive elements that went into this homepage and, overall, this was a very amusing and enjoyable experience for me.

A 10-step synopsis

Page introducing the main characters

Still cuts of scenes from the movie

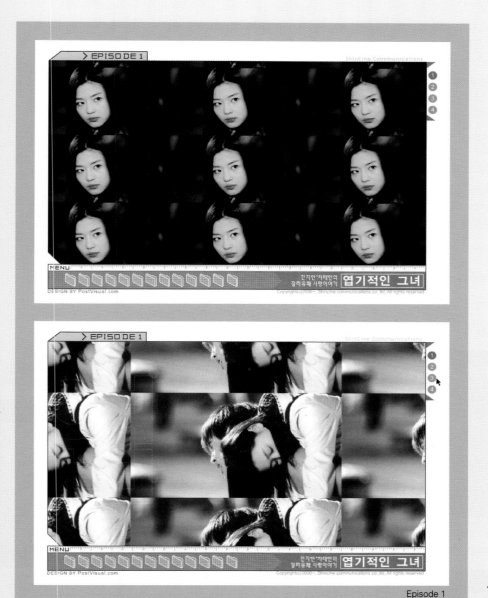

Episode 1

In the section that introduces the synopsis of the movie, the entire movie is divided into 10 stages and the users' actions cause the movie to flip from stage to stage. Of course, users who do not perform the proper action will not be able to move onto the next stage. It becomes kind of like a game. Not only can users hear the actors' voices and see clips from the movie, they are able to enjoy the homepage like a game and double their enjoyment. In the actual movie, the hero is put through many trials by the heroine, but in the homepage, the users become the targets of these ordeals to create a sense of connection to the movie. Not only is the homepage itself enjoyable, the trials themselves are quite fun.

In the section that introduces the main characters of the movie, we feel as if we have entered the personal homepage of each actor. Not only does this section introduce and describe the roles of the main characters, it also includes small Flash preview movies in the Episode menu.

The tutorial that we will go through in this chapter is an explanation of one of these Flash movies. In this movie, the main characters relive their high school days by donning their high school uniforms and dancing the night away at a disco. How many movie cuts do you think are necessary to recreate the natural dance moves seen in the movie? We will probably need anywhere from a few dozen to a few hundred cuts. However, if we use these many cuts, the file capacity will increase, preventing the movie from playing effectively on the Web. Therefore, we need to use restricted bitmap images to adequately portray the dance movements.

Diverse methods were used in this movie to create animation effects using still bitmap images. The bitmap images were repeatedly scaled down and up to create the effect of the characters moving forward and backward and the screens were rotated 360 degrees to make it appear as if the main characters were turning around. Also, the colors were altered to create the effect of changing spotlights. This effect added more life to the video clip.

Finally, a [Remix] button was made with which the users can combine the scenes created in this way. This button allows users to combine any of the 10 scenes to generate a slightly different effect each time the button is pressed.

174

Movie Applications

First, we need to open a new window and select the movie size, background color and frames per second in the [Document Properties] dialogue box. (Ctrl + J, ⌘ + J)

The frame rate used here is 30fps. A high frame rate was used to express the fast development of the movie. ("fps," which stands for "frames per second," expresses how many frames will be played per second. When still cuts are shown quickly, with short time gaps in between, they appear to be moving. The lowest frame rate that gives this effect is 8fps. Flash uses a default of 12fps.) However, just because we have made this configuration here does not mean that the movie will play at 30fps on all computers. The speed at which the movie plays depends on the CPU speed of each user's computer. For example, on computers with high performance, the movie will be played at 30fps to create the effect that the creator intended. On the other hand, computers with poorer performance will not be able to handle the overload and the movie will be played at a slower rate to give an effect unlike what the maker had intended. Therefore, how the movie is played depends on the viewer's computer speed, and the values that you configure on your computer when you make the movie are not absolute.

The [Document Properties] dialogue box

When making a movie, you must take all of these factors into consideration and select values which will allow the movie to be seen effectively on all computers. Above all, you want to be able to think of how you can most effectively relay the effect that you intended to as many users as possible.

Making Bitmap Image Scenes

The majority of the movie created here uses still cuts from the actual movie. As follows, preparing the bitmap image is very important. Because the objective here is to advertise the movie, we want to select cuts that best portray the movie itself.

[**Importing Bitmap Images and Symbolizing Them**] . . . . .

First of all, import all of the prepared bitmap images into Flash and symbolize each and every one of them. All of the sources used here are contained in the "episode2.fla" file in the supplementary CD-ROM.

1 ˙˙Sort out the bitmap images for the main actions and import
them into Flash. (Ctrl + R , ⌘ + R)

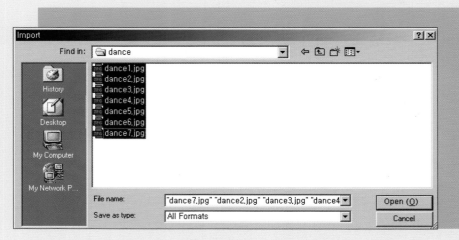

Importing bitmap images

2 When the bitmap images are all imported, they should all be piled up in the same location. We will convert them into symbols, one cut at a time. We first convert these images into symbols because we will be varying the alpha and tint values of these images later on to create diverse effects and these are options that can only be applied to symbols.

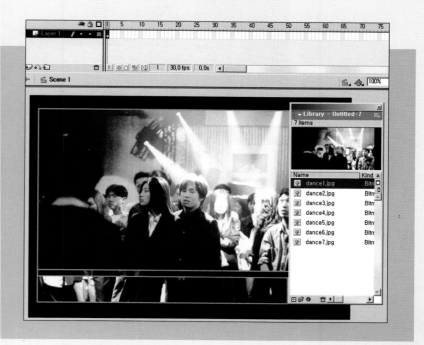

Imported images
saved in the library.

3 Select the bitmap cut at the very top.

Selecting the very first bitmap image

4 After pressing the `F8` key to open the [Symbol Properties] dialogue box, convert the image into a symbol.

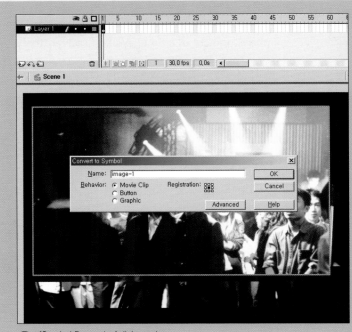

The [Symbol Properties] dialogue box

The symbols added to the library

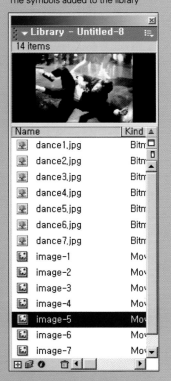

5 First delete the symbolized image from the stage and continue to symbolize the remaining images in order. When all of the images have been symbolized, they should be added to the library as shown here.

Configuring the Basic Interface · · · · ·

1 Fill up the remaining portion of the screen, excluding the area where the dance sequence will be placed with a black rectangle. This is because all of the scenes are different sizes and the boundaries are not uniform. Although we could have used masks to do the same thing, this method is much faster. (The layer in which this black rectangle has been inserted is named "black-box.")

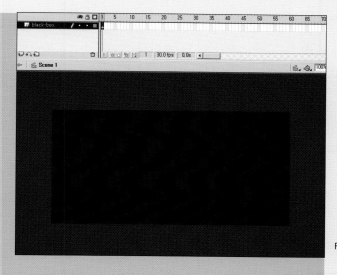

Filling in the boundaries with a black rectangle

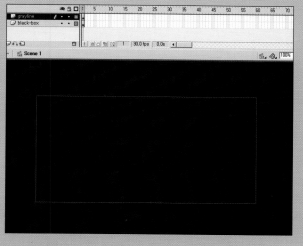

Drawing in the movie outline in the upper layer

2 After adding a layer named "grayline," make the outline around the area where the movie will be shown. This must be consistent with the boundary of the black box made in the previous step.

This step allows us to block out the areas that are not directly used to show the movie. In the next step, we will make the movie in the visible frame area.

Making the Actions 1: Spotlight Effects

We will now use the symbolized images to create the dance sequence. The first thing we need to do is to use the still cut to create a spotlight effect. Instead of using a separate spotlight cut, we can simply magnify the spotlight portion of another bitmap image.

1 ·· Make a new symbol and name it "dance1."

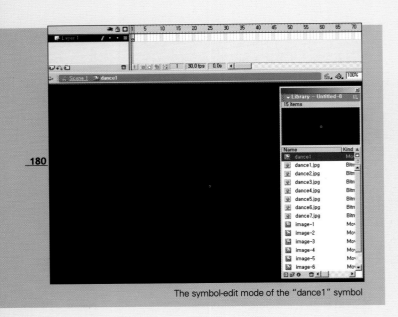

The symbol-edit mode of the "dance1" symbol

2 ·· Layout of the spotlight cut symbol, "image-3."

Layout of the "image-3" symbol

3 After adding a keyframe to frame 7, we change the overall coloring to emphasize the spotlight effect. Use the Advanced Effect feature of the Color option from the Property Inspector (Ctrl + F3 , ⌘ + F3) to adjust the color values. We can brighten the overall color by raising the value on the right side.

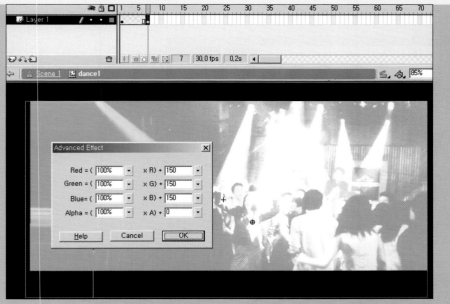

After making a keyframe in frame 7, adjusting the color using the Advanced Effect feature of the Color option from the Property Inspector

4 Motion tween frames between 1-7. This completes the step of brightening the bitmap image.

Motion tween frames between 1 - 7

5 After adding a layer, use the "image-1" symbol to brighten the color of frames 8-19 in the same way.

Altering the color values after adding a frame to frames 8 through 19

6 Using the same method described above, still cuts were used to create changing spotlight effects. There's no need to worry that the outline of the movie is not consistent. This can be taken care of when we lay out the symbol in the movie-edit mode.

[　**Making the Actions 2: Dance Sequence Using Guide Layers**　] . . . . .

We will use Guide Layers to make the characters appear like they are dancing. I put a lot of thought into how I could use still cuts to make the characters appear like they're dancing. The following is one of the solutions that I found.

1 ˙˙ Make a new symbol and name it "dance2."

2 ˙˙ Lay out the "image-4" symbol on the stage.

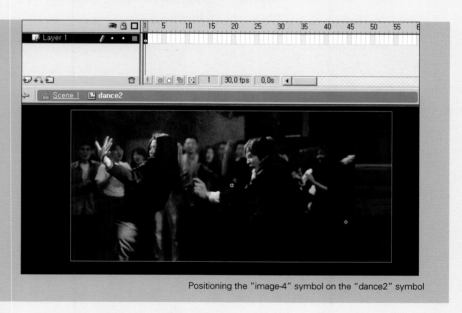

Positioning the "image-4" symbol on the "dance2" symbol

3 ** Click the "Add a Guide Layer" icon to add a layer.

Adding a Guide Layer

4 ** After selecting the Pencil Tool from the toolbox, which will be used to draw the outline, select the "Smooth" option.

Selecting the "Smooth" option

5 Select the Guide Layer and draw a slow curve. (In order to prevent this guideline from transforming during the rest of the process, it is a good to lock the layer.)

Drawing a "U-shaped" curve

6 Now we will have the symbol motion tweening along this guideline. A (+) sign will appear in the middle of the symbol when it is selected. Bring this to the point where the guideline begins. When doing this, select the Magnet Tool from the toolbox and adjust the position of the image so that a small circle appears when the symbol and the action guideline approach each other. The two will then stick together. In the same way, arrange the center point of the image on the starting point of the curve. (If this is difficult to understand, refer to the "dance2" movie clip of the "episode2.fla" file in the supplementary CD-ROM.)

The point where the guideline begins

After selecting the Magnet Tool, the center point of the image is arranged on the starting point of the guideline.

7 After making a keyframe in frame 8, position the symbol on the other end. The (+) sign on the center point of the image and the end point of the action guideline must fall precisely into place.

8 Motion tween frames between 1-8. To add acceleration, set the Easing value to "-100." This creates a tweening that gets gradually faster.

Specifying a motion tweening with an Ease value of "-100" to frames 1 - 8

186

tip >>

What is Ease?

Ease is an option that adds acceleration to tweening. For example, to create movements that get gradually faster, select a negative Ease value and to create movements that get gradually slower, select a positive Ease value. This adds elasticity to the tweening and creates more vivid movements.

9 We have now completed the movement of the symbol moving from left to right. Now we will make the movement that moves from right to left.

10 After making a keyframe in frame 15, move the symbol to the right.

11 Motion tween frames 8 - 15 and set the Ease value to "100."

Specifying a motion tweening with an Ease value of "100" to frames 8 - 15

12 We have now completed the action that moves from side to side following the action guidelines drawn in the Guide Layer.

Making the Actions 3: Revolutions · · · · ·

We will now create the action where the lead male backspins spectacularly on the floor. This, however, does not actually appear in the movie. The leading man in the movie only attempts to try it, but doesn't quite succeed. However, in Flash, we will rotate the still cut 360 degrees to make it appear as if the lead male has successfully completed the backspin. This scene is an example of where I used my imagination to create dance sequences using various still cuts from the movie.

1 Make a new symbol and name it "dance5."

2 Lay out the "image-5" symbol on the stage.

Arranging the "image-5" symbol on the "dance5" symbol

3 Make a keyframe in frame 10.

4 Motion tween frames 1-10 with the Ease value set to "-100." Have the lead make one clockwise revolution.

Having the leading man make one clockwise revolution, the frames 1-10 were motion tweened with the Ease value set to "-100."

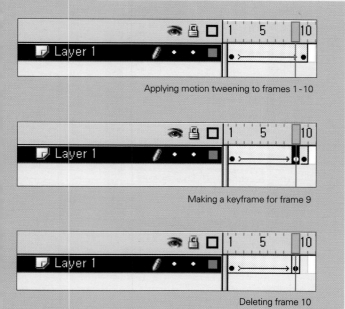

Applying motion tweening to frames 1-10

Making a keyframe for frame 9

Deleting frame 10

5 However, this makes the action in frames 1 and 10 identical. Therefore, make a keyframe in frame 9 (F6) and delete frame 10. (Shift + F6)

6 By deleting this last frame, we can repeat the frames as many times as we wish and still end up with a natural action.

Making an Action 4: Changing the Size of the Image

This action is very simple. All we need to do is to take the same image and just alter the size and use it for two animation frames. However, we can create very amusing effects by altering the color of this symbol in the movie-edit mode. Rapidly increasing and decreasing images make the characters appear as if they are dancing with fervor.

1 ·· Make a new symbol and name it "dance6."

2 ·· Lay out the "image-6" symbol on the stage.

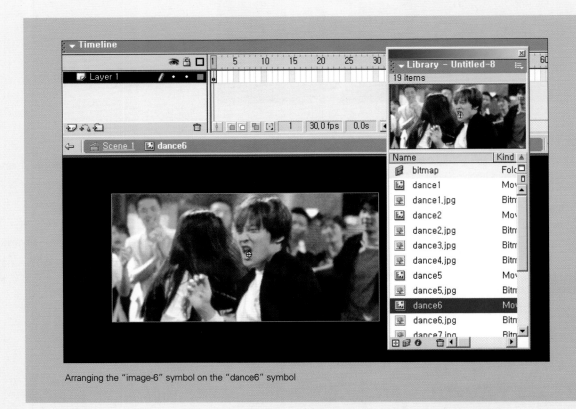

Arranging the "image-6" symbol on the "dance6" symbol

3 After making a keyframe in frame 2, raise the scale of the image to 120% in the [Scale and Rotate] window ([Modify]-[Transform]-[Scale & Rotate]).

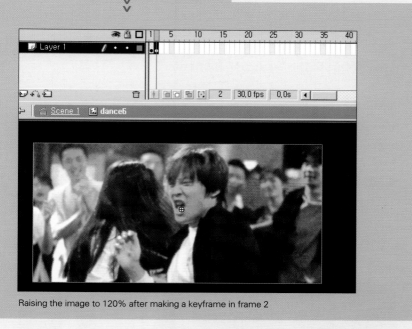

Raising the image to 120% after making a keyframe in frame 2

All the remaining actions have been made in the same way, so I will refrain from going through all the explanations here. These actions will then be arranged in the movie-edit mode.

Arranging in the Movie-Edit Mode

The first part of the movie, where the main characters enter the nightclub, was made using motion tweening with alpha values. For more details, refer to the "episode2.fla" file in the supplementary CD-ROM. In this section, we will look at where the actions begin.

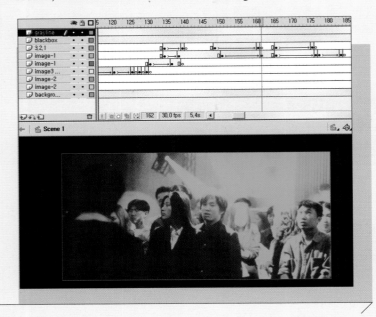

Adding the movie to the beginning of the movie. (We will not go over this area here so refer to the supplementary CD-ROM.)

[**Laying Out of the "dance1" Symbol**] • • • • •

1 •• After adding a layer (a: dance1), position the "dance1" symbol where the dance action begins, frame 185.

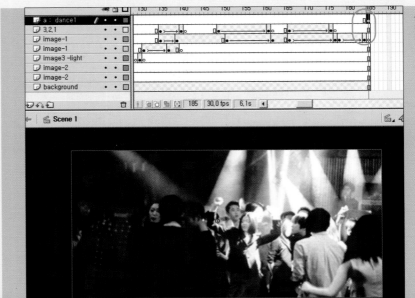

Arranging the "dance1" symbol in the added layer, frame185

2 Because we will be emphasizing the spotlights in this scene, we increase the size of the symbol.

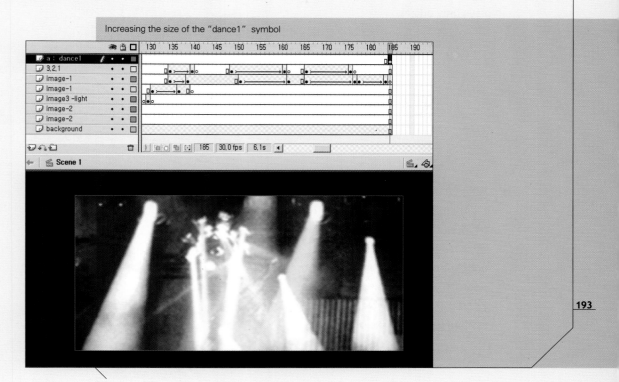

Increasing the size of the "dance1" symbol

3 Right now, the symbol "Behavior" option is set to "Movie Clip." However, this movie clip has the disadvantage that the actions will not appear in Flash, but only in swf files. Therefore, we change the "Behavior" option to "Graphic" symbol to verify the action in Flash. We need to change the "Movie Clip" symbol to a "Graphic" symbol in order to verify the actions in Flash.

4 After selecting the "dance1" symbol, open the Property Inspector. (Ctrl + F3 , ⌘ + F3)

5 Change the "Behavior" option to "Graphic." Then, check the "Play once" option. (The "Play once" option ensures that the symbol plays only once.)

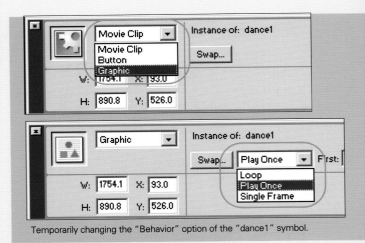

Temporarily changing the "Behavior" option of the "dance1" symbol.

6 After changing to "Graphic" symbol, add a frame [F5] and verify the action. Add a frame so that the symbol is played once. Because this symbol is used in a 19-frame animation in the symbol-editing mode, we need to add a total of 19 frames. After adding frames up to frame 204, play the symbol to verify the movement.

Changing the "Behavior" option to "Graphic" allows us to see the action in Flash

Adding frames up to frame 204

7 After playing the action, use the ⟨F7⟩ key to add an empty keyframe to frame 205 to end the action. If the action is not stopped, the animation will continue to loop. Of course, we could have simply selected "Play Once" instead of "Loop" in the [Instance] panel, but since we will be adding an action right after this one, we use the first method instead.

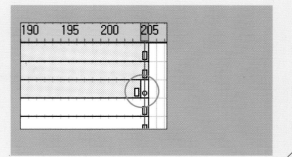

195

tip ⌄⌄

The Difference Between Graphic and Movie Clip Symbols
(Refer to the "movie-graphic.fla" file in the supplementary CD-ROM.)

1. Movie Clip Symbol

The movie clip is an independent movie. Therefore, animations made as a movie clip will play regardless as to the number of frames in the main movie.

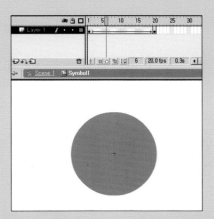

❶ Frames 1-20 have been motion-tweened in the symbol-editing mode of the movie clip symbol.

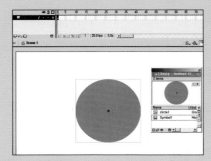

❷ After converting to the movie-editing mode, drag the movie clip symbol from the library onto the stage. The movie clip is added to frame 1.

❸ Pressing the [Enter] key to play the movie, we can see no visible differences.

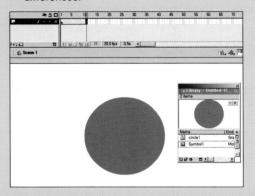

Some users may feel that this is because this movie is made up of only one frame. However, no matter how many frames we add, we still have no action. The fact that there is no movement is not unusual, however. This is because we cannot see the actions of movie clips in Flash. We can only see the action when it is changed into an "swf" file.

❹ We can see the actions of the movie clip by changing it into an "swf" file by selecting [Test Movie]. ([Ctrl] + [Enter])

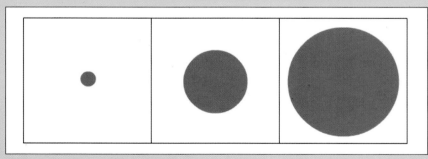

Playing the movie in the [Test Movie] mode

The entire animation of the movie clip will appear in the main movie if it is more than one frame long. The movie clip is an independent movie that can play the animation in only one frame.

2. Graphic Symbol

Graphic symbols are used frequently in still images. Of course, animations are possible in graphic symbols, but they differ from movie clip symbols in that they are limited by the number of frames in the main movie. Therefore, if you want to control the movie based on the number of frames in the main movie, graphic symbols are the more convenient choice. We will now look into what it means to be controlled by the main frame.

❶ The following is an animation of the graphic symbol in frames 1-20.

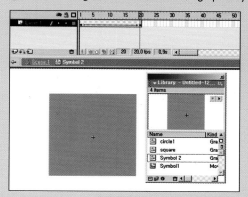

❷ After converting to the movie-edit mode, drag the symbol from the library and situate it on the stage.

❸ Add frames until there are a total of 10 frames. (This is done by selecting frame 10 with the mouse and pressing the (F5) key.)

❹ Pressing the (Enter) key to play the movie, we can see that there is movement in frames 1-10.

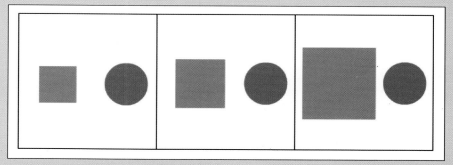

Only graphic symbols show movement in Flash.

⑤ Changing to an "swf" file will still show movement in frames 1-10. However, the movie clip symbol will show movement in frames 1-20.

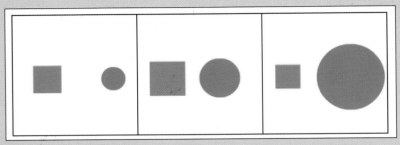

Changing to an "swf" file, the graphic symbol will only show movement in the number of frames in the main movie, but the movie clip symbol will show the entire animation.

Thus, we see that graphic symbols are affected by the number of frames in the main movie. This is in contrast to the movie clip symbol, which will show movement even in only one frame.

3. Configuring the "Behavior" Option of the Symbol

The "Behavior" option, which is configured in the [Symbol Properties] dialogue box when the symbol is first made, can be changed at any time as needed. As we saw earlier, movie clip symbols are independent movies that are not restricted by the number of frames in the main movie, but have the disadvantage that the actions cannot be seen in Flash. Therefore, after arranging the movie clip symbol on the stage, we can change the "Behavior" option to "Graphic" to verify the movement. We do this in the following way:

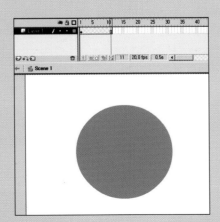

❶ Lay out the movie clip symbol on the stage.

❷ In the Property Inspector, change the "Behavior" option to "Graphic." Then, change the "Graphic" option to "Loop" or "Play once." (The "Loop" option will have the movie play over and over again depending on the number of main frames and the "Play once" option will have the movie play only once, despite the number of main frames.)

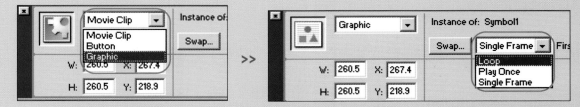

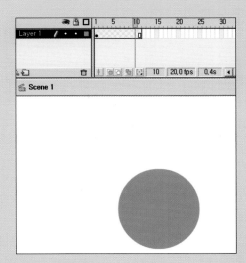

Changing the "Behavior" option to "Graphic" allows us to play the animation in Flash.

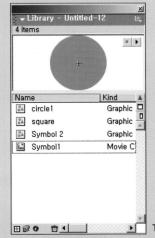

However, switching the "Behavior" option of the movie clip symbol to "Graphic" does not change the basic behavior of the symbol. Looking in the library, we see that this symbol is still classified as a "movie clip symbol." This change in the "Behavior" option is only a temporary instance when the symbol is selected.

The symbol is not changed in the library.

Laying Out the "dance2" Symbol

• • • • •

Now we will position the "dance2" symbol and then change the color values in the [Effect] panel to make it appear as if the spotlight is changing.

1 Make a new layer (b: dance2) and then make a keyframe in frame 205.

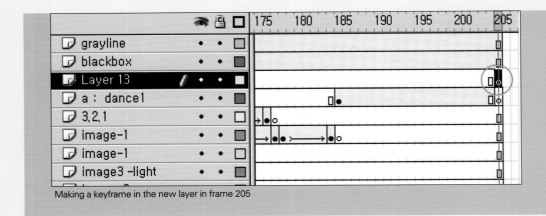

Making a keyframe in the new layer in frame 205

2 Position the "dance2" symbol.

Arranging the "dance2" symbol

3 ·· In the [Instance] panel of the "dance2" symbol, set the "Behavior" to "Graphic" and then select "Loop."

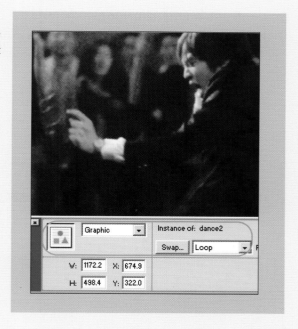

4 ·· Add frames until frame 249 so that the symbol is made to loop three times. This is done by selecting frame 249 and pressing the ⌧F5 key.

5 ·· The first frames of the looping action are made using keyframes (⌧F6).

Making a keyframe for the first frame of the looping action

6 ¨Configure a different color value for each of the keyframes. After selecting the symbol of the respective frame, adjust the RGB values under "Advanced" in the [Effect] panel.

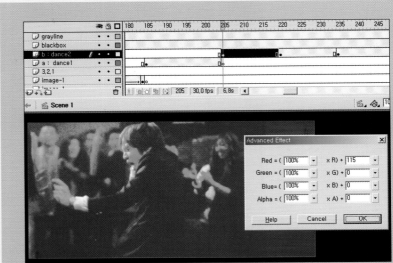

Changing the color of the first loop

Changing the color of the second loop

202

06. Episode from the Movie *My Sassy Girl*

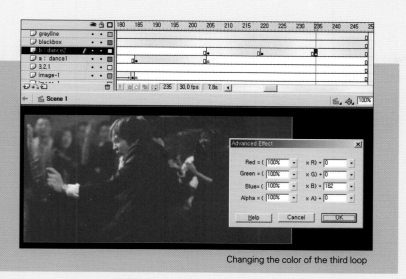

Changing the color of the third loop

7 By doing this, it will appear as if the color of the spotlight is changing while the characters are dancing.

Using the same method, we can arrange the other actions, one by one, in the movie-editing mode. It is even better if the actions are combined in keeping with the overall rhythm of the movie.

Making the [Movie Remix] Button

This movie as it is, when exported as an "swf" file, will play according to the time sequence. The other symbols can be arranged in the same way in the movie-edit mode. However, I thought that it would be fun to allow users to control the actions themselves. This was done by attaching a label to the frame with action and allowing it to be controlled by a button.

[**Assigning a Label to the Frame**] . . . . .

The button will be given the action to go and play each action frame and each of the frames will have a label that displays this. (This label will not change even though the name of the frame is changed or modified.)

Although we can use the frame numbers for the action, it is much more convenient to use a frame label than to go looking for each frame number. For example, if we were to use frame numbers, if the movie sequence were to move back by one frame, we would have to go back and reassign all the frame numbers again. On the other hand, labels are absolute and are a very good choice to use in movies, which can change and be modified at any time. And, anyway, isn't it better to enter "a,b..." rather than "386, 259..." in the action window.

1 Make a new layer (frame label) and add a keyframe to the first action frame where the "dance1" symbol is situated (frame 186).

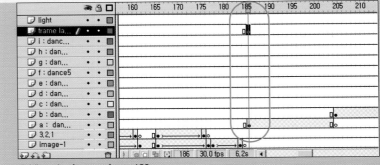

Adding a keyframe to frame 186

2 After selecting the "Frame Label" layer of frame 186, enter an "a" in the label line in the Property Inspector.

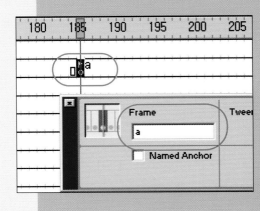

3 A red flag and the letter "a" will appear in the frame.

4 In the same way, add labels (in alphabetical order) to the first frames of each new action. Although you can choose any name you want for the labels, because label names also affect the file size, it is better to choose a very simple name.

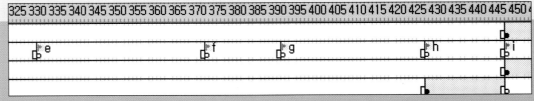

Adding a label to the first frames of each new action

[**Movie Remix**] . . . . .

Now we will have these frames controlled by a button.

1 After adding a layer to the very top, make a button symbol. As shown in the following illustration, in making the button, the Up frame is left blank and a circle is drawn in the over frame.

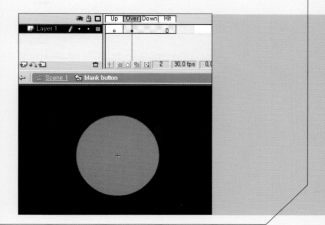

2 Because the Up frame was left blank, when it is arranged in the movie-edit mode, only a transparent blue form will appear. Create as many buttons as there are types of actions and then lay them out. In order to evenly space the buttons, use the [Align] window. (Ctrl + K , ⌘ + K)

If the button does not appear transparent and blue, it means that the button is activated. To inactivate the button, undo the [Control]-[Enable Simple Button] command. (Ctrl + Alt + B , ⌘ + option + B)

Because the Up frame was left blank, the buttons in the main movie will appear blue and transparent.

Assigning a "GoTo" Action to the Button · · · · ·

We will add the "Move to frame label a and play" action to the first button.

1 ·· After selecting the button, open the [Object Actions] window.

Selecting the button and
opening the action window

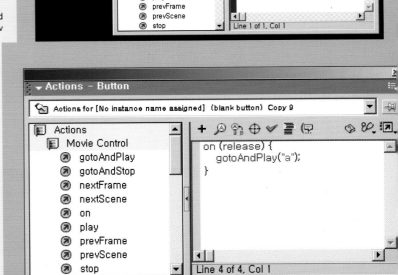

2 ·· Enter the following action script:

```
on (release){
        gotoAndPlay("a");
}
```

Assigning the "Move to frame label a and play" action

3 ·· Now, when this button is pressed, the movie will begin playing from frame label "a."

4 ·· Use the same method to add actions to go to the other remaining labels for the other buttons.

5 ·· Finally, all we need to do is to number the buttons for user convenience.

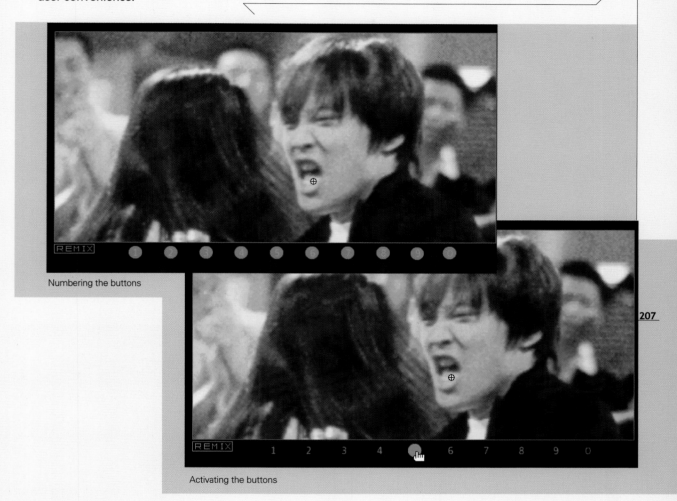

Numbering the buttons

Activating the buttons

6 ·· Select [Test Movie]. The movie will play in order until one of the buttons is pressed. This will have the movie begin playing from the respective frame label.

In this chapter, we observed how to effectively use still bitmap images to portray action and how to control frames using buttons. These have all been designed to fit the concept of the film. Although this dance sequence is only a small portion of the actual movie, the user will have a chance to watch and control the wild dance of the main characters.

Jens Schmidt

www.yenz.com

1. What do you think of "Motion Graphics"?

Motion Graphics are the extension of the static information. They have a great potential to raise the user's emotion. They are not always the straightest way to transport information but they always attract the user's attention.

Animated sites mark the Internet of today, but not all animations are done with a lot of skill. Some animation is done nicely, but when they are over you may ask yourself what the purpose was to do them. They are like flickering images with short-term effects. Animating something does not legitimize a missing message but on the other hand I would prefer a nicely done animation instead of a boring message.

2. Could you tell me what are some features that stand out in your own works involving "Motion Graphics"?

For me it is important that the sequence of images the animation consists of build together one floating composition. Even if you do not see clearly every single image, you feel that there is something wrong in the end if it is not done in the right way. Things that transform, file size and change of color are very important issues in the creation of animation for the web.

3. Please tell me about both advantages and disadvantages of "Flash Motion Graphics"?

Flash allows you to tell stories which can bee seen all over the world via Internet with a relatively small effort spent on the production of the film. This is definitively a big advantage of Flash because it allows a great number of people to enter the field of narrative storytelling they might never have discovered otherwise.
The disadvantage of Flash is the slowness of animations if you use transparency effects and the decreasing performance if you animate several things simultaneously.

4. These days, I think another issue in the Web is "Interaction." Feel free to talk about Interaction.

Interaction is the most important issue of the Internet and the most particular difference to linear films. The interaction gives the user a chance to become active and to contribute something to an application. He can feel creative and discover things instead of being a passive consumer. Interaction is nice and sometimes it is a lot of work but it is worth it because it prolongs the cycle of existence of an application.

Jens Schmidt

Flash MX Motion Graphics

07. The Similarity Between You & I

You think life is beautiful.
And you like sky blue, cafe au lait, nachos.
Do you need love? I wish you have it.
The similarity between You & I is 72%.
But, It is just a number, it isn't important to us.
Anyway, I am happy to meet you.

Concept

I started this project in hopes of testing the oneness between myself and the anonymous user. The funny thing is that these percents change from time to time and when all the questions are asked, these numbers speak to me.

You and I are 55% similar!!! You like cappuccino? Me too. I especially like my cappuccino with cinnamon sprinkled on top.

Isn't that interesting?

In *The Little Prince*, there is one line that states that adults like numbers. Rather than simply stating "I met her a long time ago", they like to say "I saw her standing 100M in front of me about 2-3 months ago at around 5 o'clock." Is this the same thing? Is it just a fancy that the similarity between people can be brought down to a percent value? In reality, it is not possible to gain an accurate picture of the similarity between me and another person simply by asking a few questions. However, I wanted to pursue this thread of conversation so that I could feel the similarity between me and the other person. Instead of the one-directional "one person receives/one person gives" kind of setup, I want an ideal and equal interaction where I give half and the user gives half.

A Sensitive Interaction!

This is something that, I believe, the Internet should continue to strive for. For the users who are worn out by the continuous outpouring of information from the Web, I want to strive towards maintaining that serious connection and communication between users, and this project is an extent of that desire.

The first question that this project asks is "Do you think life is beautiful?" (How about you? How would you answer this question?)

My questions start with topics that everyone can relate to, such as "Are you alive?" or "Can you think right now?" I did this in order to set the user at ease. Then, when the user answers "Yes," "No" or "So-so," I respond in kind. For instance, users who answered "Yes" get +10%, those who answered "No" get 2% and those who answered "So-so" get -10%. These are predetermined values that I have setup. In this way, as the people respond to these questions, they affect the percentage of "similarity" between us.

When this question is answered, another one follows.

"Do you like cheese on your nachos?"
"(Listening to music) Do you know the title of this song?"
"Choosing from love, money, time and rest, what is the one thing that you need the most right now?"
"What kind of coffee do you like?"

In order to prevent these questions from becoming boring, sights and sounds were used and the tempo of the entire project was adjusted.

After a few more questions, a final similarity percentage is shown and a discussion is held on the results.
This is the final step in this process.

You think Life is beautiful.
And you like sky blue, cafe au lait, nachos.
Do you need love? I pray you find it.
The similarity between You & I is 72%.
But, it is just a number, it isn't important to us.
Anyway, it was nice meeting you.

Orange Color is added to the window to draw attention.

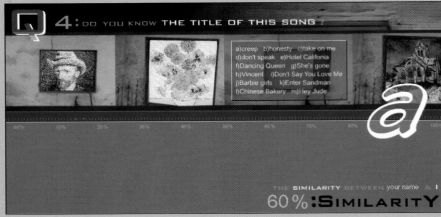

In this section, a piece of music will be heard and the user must identify the name of the song. Images related music will be framed and put on display.

The concept behind this design is "Many Windows."

This is because in order to effectively arrange the many questions and their respective images, an interface that allows flexibility within the standard frame is necessary.

Looking at the layout, we can see that the stage is divided along the horizontal. At the top, there are the images for each question and at the bottom is the percentage value that changes with each answer to the questions. As the image in the top frame is continuously changing with the questions, the bottom frame remains mostly blank.

Providing a frame for rest, while the other one is continuously changing, reflects the extent of the designer's thoroughness and attention to detail, much like the "Beauty of Empty Space" that is seen in many Asian paintings.

This section asks the question. "What kind of coffee do you like?" The entire screen was colored in brown tones to match the mood of the question.

In terms of color as well, if the top portion is a continuously shifting panorama of color, the bottom frame should be slightly muted with monotones. Also, in order to prevent the bottom space from flowing out, type is used to fix the attention on this frame.

The "a" in the "answer" is made into a transparent 3D image to change the vertical and horizontal viewpoint, and an actual photograph, converted to a bitmap image, was used for the window in order to emphasize the density seen by vector images. In particular, the window was used to effectively restructure the screen.

In the first question, only the color of the image was changed to hold the user's attention and certain details are given in order to maintain the ambience of the question, i.e. a brown color for the coffee question and a framed Van Gogh painting.

Using images in this way to create diverse effects is extremely useful in maintaining the unity of a project.

As mentioned above, this project was designed to give a changing percent value based on a question/answer interaction. The answer choices are represented by buttons and actions must be given to these buttons so that they can control other elements.

1 After selecting the Text Tool, enter the number "0" on the stage. Then, after selecting the text, increase the font size under Text Options in the Property Inspector. This panel can also be used to modify the color or text alignment.

216

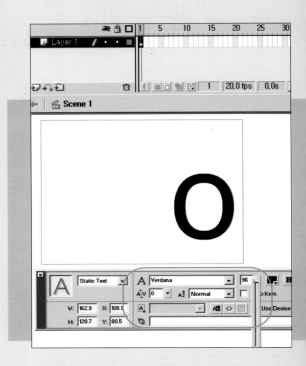

2 In the Property Inspector, change the Text Type to "Dynamic Text."

3 Enter "zero" in the Variable line. This makes the variable "0." Another number can be selected.

Now the text field will act like the "zero" variable.

tip >>

Adjust the text field so that it can accommodate values up to three places and right-align it.
This is so that it can represent similarity from 0 - 100 %.

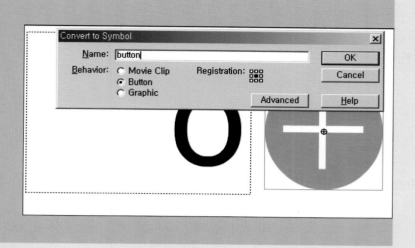

4 Make a ⊕ object and convert it into a button symbol by selecting [Insert] - [Convert to Symbol] (You can also use the "button" symbol in the "Similarity-b.fla" library on the CD-ROM.)

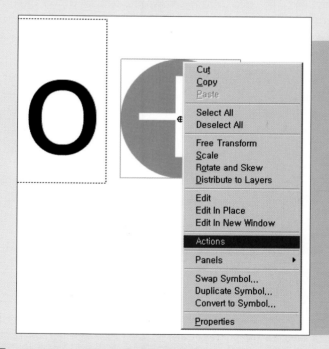

5 After selecting the "button" symbol on the stage, open the [Actions] panel. (F9)

Looking at the other options under [Text Type]

Several options can be saved in the Text as you need them.
They are, as follows:

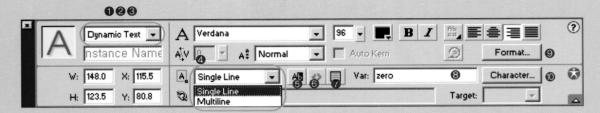

❶ **Static text**: This option converts the text into an image file when it is exported to swf. The font selected in the fla file is maintained in the anti-aliasing format.

❷ **Dynamic text**: This option maintains the characteristics of the text as it is exported. If the selected font does not exist on the other person's computer, the font either changes or will not show up. Therefore, it is recommended that common fonts, such as arial, helvetica and courier, are used.

❸ **Input text**: This option is similar to dynamic text. When this option is selected, it allows the user to enter the text directly into the text window when exporting. This option also contains a password function, which encrypts the text when it is entered. The max characters function can also be used to limit the text length.

❹ **Single Line, Multiline or Multiline No Wrap**: This option allows us to decide whether we will express the text in Multiline or Single Line when the text is longer than the text window. Multiline No Wrap is an option that does not automatically cause the text to change lines according to the size of the text box.

❺ **Selectable**: Allows the user to select the text when exporting.

❻ **HTML**: This option allows us to specify whether the text will be displayed in HTML format. If this option is selected, many colors and fonts can be used within one text window.

❼ **Border/Bg**: This allows us to hide or display the borders of the text.

❽ **Var (Variable)**: This is where we enter the values for the text field. The text field is then controlled by actions according to the value entered here.

❾ **Format**: Used to adjust the indent, line spacing, left/right margin, etc.

❿ **Character**: Character is used to create the embedded option of the font. "Embedded" means that when the file is exported as an swf file, the font is exported at the same time.

Variable: The name of the specified variable.
Value: The value assigned to the variable.

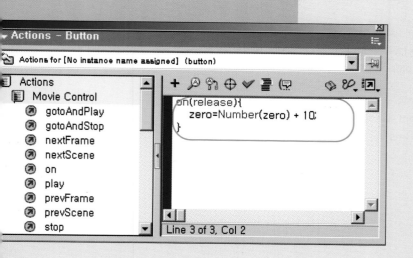

6 This will cause the following script to appear. This script states that when the button is released (clicked), a value of 10 will be added to the variable "zero." Here is the complete script:

```
on (release) {
        zero = Number(zero) + 10;
}
```

219

You should be realizing at this point just how simple the action script that is used in this project is. Now we will learn how to utilize and apply this basic source to a an actual project.

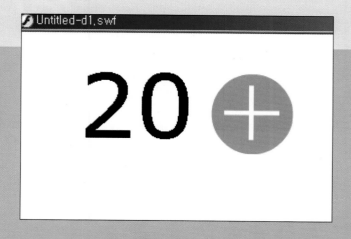

After selecting [Control] - [Test Movie] and clicking the button, we can see the numbers in the test field increase by intervals of 10.

This project repeats the same action script over and over again, because the same action is used after every question. Therefore, we will take this basic action apart and observe it closely.

- Making a text field with a user name.
- Making an answer-sensitive percent window.
- Making a document based on the answers.

Input Text

In the first screen, the user will see a text field with the words, "WRITE YOUR NAME IN THE ORANGE BOX". Entering one's own name in the text field will produce the following screen. This portion represents the "YOU" factor in the "THE SIMILARITY BETWEEN YOU & I" and was created to foster a more friendly atmosphere.

While the user enters his or her name in the designated text field, the name will appear simultaneously in the text field at the bottom

[**Making the Input Text Field**] · · · · ·

1 ·· Enter "your name" in the text field.

2 ·· After selecting this text field, set the Text Type to "Input Text" in the Property Inspector and enter the variable "name" for "Var."

tip >>

Setting the Text Type to "Input Text" allows users to enter text directly in the Web form when it's converted to an swf file.

3 ·· Make a copy of this and place one directly below. We can see the real time relay of the text written in the swf file to the bottom. Here, the size of the text does not matter because text fields with the same variable name will always have the same contents.

A text field with the same variable name

Value Display Text

Before moving on, let's think about why we are doing this.

For the first question, THINK LIFE IS BEAUTIFUL? there are buttons for the three possible answers: Yes, I think so; Well...I'm not sure; No, I don't think so. Clicking on each will result in the respective action.

Then I will configure a +, - value for each button.

First of all, I think life is well worth living; sometimes its beautiful, sometimes its not.

Yes, I think so —————————— +3
Well... I'm not sure —————— +5
No, I don't think so ————— -5

All I have done is to convert my own opinions into numbers. Then, when the user replies to the questions, the numbers will fluctuate accordingly. Through these numbers, we will find out how alike we are.

222

[**Making an Answer - Sensitive Percent Window**] . . . . .

1 After making the text field, enter the value "50" to stand for 50%. This is because we will start at 50% and add actions that will cause this number to go up or down +, -10 based on the answers to the questions.

First, we will configure the text field at the bottom that displays the "%"

223

2 After specifying Text Type to "Dynamic Text" in the Property Inspector, set the variable to "fifty."

Above, we made a default text field with the variable name "fifty" that stands for 50%. We will now add actions that will cause this number to go up or down +, -10 based on the answers.

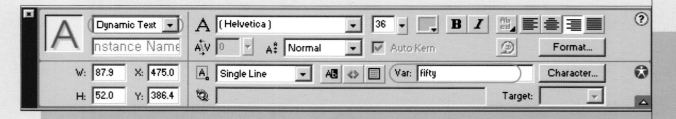

3 We will make transparent buttons for each of the replies. The method we used here is to place a transparent button over the reply and instill each button with the respective action. These buttons were created without an Up frame. Of course, we could have made a different button for each reply, but the transparent button is a more practical choice because the size can be adjusted to be used most anywhere.

A transparent button made for the empty "Up" frame

tip >>

A transparent button is one that does not have an object in the Up frame and becomes transparent when there is no mouse action. This transparent button is made so that the background color changes when the mouse is placed over the button. After making the symbol button as shown here, all we have to do is to situate the semi-transparent rectangular object in the Over frame.

4 After situating the transparent button on the reply,
make the individual action scripts:

❶ Yes, I think so.

```
on (release) {
        fifty = Number(fifty) + 3
}
```

❷ Well... I'm not sure.

```
on (release) {
        fifty = Number(fifty) + 5
}
```

❸ No, I don't think so.

```
on (release) {
        fifty = Number(fifty) - 5
}
```

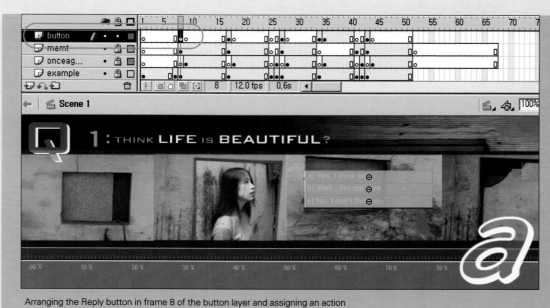

Arranging the Reply button in frame 8 of the button layer and assigning an action

In the same way, after specifying values for the other questions, we make the configurations so
that the results are put on display right away.

5 One other thing that we need to add to each button is the "go to nextframe" action script that will make it jump to the next frame. This prevents the user from trying to answer two questions at once. Once the question is answered, the user is jumped to the next frame and the previous question cannot be changed. If previous answers can be changed, it can cause repetitive answers and confuse the percentage operation.

6 Add the following action scripts for each of the replies:

```
on (release) {
    nextFrame ();
}
```

Now, each of the buttons has been endowed with an action, one action to do a +, - calculation in the fifty field and one action that moves to the next frame.

7 All we need to do for the next frame is to erase the button and make a "Next" button that will take the user to the next frame.

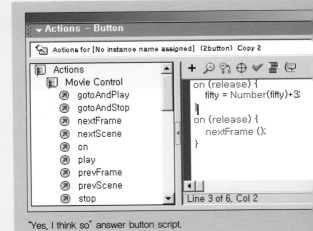

"Yes, I think so" answer button script.

When the reply is selected, the user should be taken immediately to the next frame (Figure ❶). However, in order to prevent the question from being answered twice, the reply button is removed from the next frame and instead a NEXT button is made to take the user to the next question (Figure ❷)

Figure ❶

Figure ❷

Once the user finishes answering all the questions, a document pertaining to the previous replies will be created in the last screen. This document shows in greater detail the similarities between me and the user and was created to foster a feeling of camaraderie between the two of us.

There are many possibilities but each user will end up with one result. This is the most meaningful element in the creation of my one-to-one conversation. I did not want to create a limited interaction whereby the users move to the linked page by simply clicking a button, but a more developed interaction where the results change based on the users' reactions.

Glance at the Structure of the Final Results

Let's first take a look at the final outcome. The text shown in green shows answers that will change depending on the question, and the word in each was used as the variable name for each text frame. The answers to the first question will appear in the area marked (Life).

Looking at this so far, it's not any different from the value calculation we made earlier. However, the values this time are in the form of sentences and for each reply, there is a corresponding word or sentence. For example, depending on the reply, (Life) is going to be filled in with the following:

You think life is (life).
And you like(color), (coffee), (nachos).
Do you need (thing)? I pray you find it.
The similarity between You & I is (fifty)%.
But, it is just a number, it isn't important to us.
Anyway, it was nice meeting you.

Yes, I think so _____beautiful.
Well...I'm not sure _____ not bad.
No, I don't think so _____ not beautiful.

For example, if the user replies, "No, I don't think so," then the last line will read, "You think life is not beautiful."

We need to do two things in order to get this response.

227

Making the Outcome for Questions and Answers that Match

. . . . .

1 First, let's make the data that will be displayed as the action script in the final result. After making a text field with the "Dynamic Text" option, the variable name is set to "life." Because this is not the area that will appear on the screen, we place it outside the window.

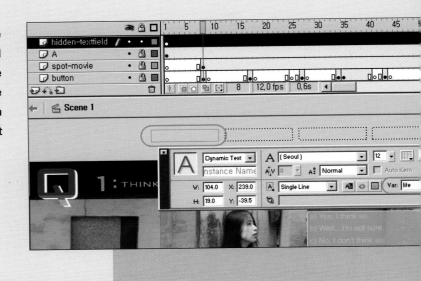

228

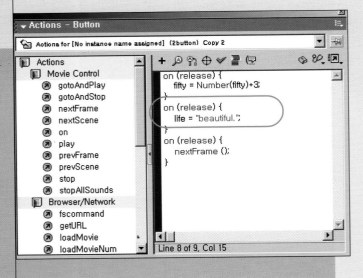

2 Add the following action script for the "Yes, I think so" reply button:

```
on (release) {
    life = "beautiful.";
}
```

This script means that the text "beautiful" has been entered for the "life" text field.

3 Using the method above, fill in the respective text fields for the remaining questions and then apply the actions for each reply button. Applying this script, when the first question is answered, the respective text will appear in the "life" text field. Although we cannot see this now, it will be used when the final results are tabulated in the end.

Using the method above, fill in the respective text fields for the remaining questions and then apply the actions for each reply button. I will refrain from explaining it again here, but if you have any questions, refer to the "similarity.fla" file on the CD-ROM.

We will now add an action to the last button that will tabulate all the replies into a text form after all the questions have been answered. Before doing that, let's look at the rule for displaying texts with variable texts.

In the first question, "You think life is (life)", depending on the user's reply, the respective text will appear in the space, (life).
As follows, different variables will appear in the text field depending on the answers to the questions.

You think life is (life)
➡ "You think life is" + life + newline +

And you like (color), (coffee), (nachos)
➡ "And you like" + color +", "+ coffee + ", "+ nachos

Using these generalizations to make the script, we get the following:

You think life is (life)
And you like (color), (coffee), (nachos)
Do you need (thing)? I wish you have it.
The similarity between You & I is (fifty)%.
But, it is just a number, it isn't important to us.
Anyway, I am happy to meet you.

➡ "You think life is " + life + newline + "And you like " + color +",
    " + coffee + ", " + nachos + newline + "Do you need " + thing + "?
    I wish you have it." + newline + "The similarity between You & I is
    " + fifty + "%" + newline + "But, it is just a number, it isn't
    important to us." + newline + "Anyway, I am happy to meet you."

An example of a text that was created using this process is seen here.
(This example text was color-coded for easier understanding. An actual script will not
be color-coded.)

> You think life is not bad.
> And you like yellow, capuccino, nachos.
> Do you need money? I wish you have it.
> The similarity between You & I is 73%.
> But, it is just a number, it isn't important to us.
> Anyway, I am happy to meet you.

Now we are going to add action to the last button that links to the text field that was
created using the method above.

1 Enter the following action script for the [NEXT] button
of the final question:

230

```
on (release) {
    last = "You think life is " + life + newline +
    "And you like " + color + "," + coffee + ", "
    + nachos + newline + "Do you need " + thing
    + "? I wish you have it." + newline +
    "The similarity between You & I is " + fifty + "%."
    + newline + "But, it is just a number, it isn't important to us."
    + newline + "Anyway, I am happy to meet you.";
}
```

The button that takes us to the final screen.

2 Add the "go to" action that will move the user to the last frame. Here, the label was given a value of "end" and moved.

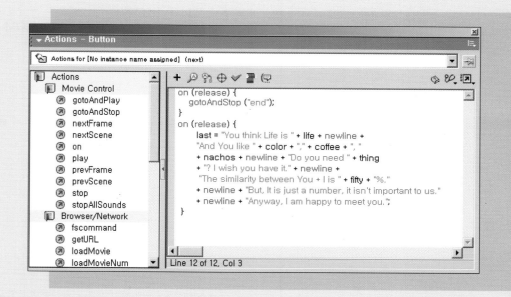

3 We will make a text field with the variable name "last" in the last scene to which we jumped. Then the font size, type and color are chosen.

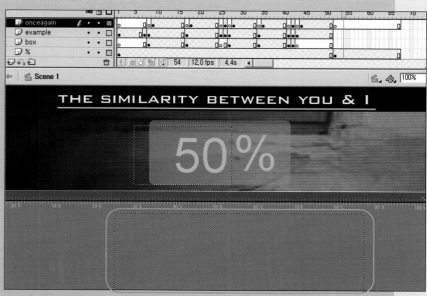

Situation of the text field that has the variable name "last" in the final screen

This will create an interactive project that displays the changing percentage values in text form. The most important thing here was the link to the text field. This connection can be adapted in many ways.

I have included the project "THE SIMILARITY BETWEEN YOU & I", in the Interaction section at www.seoleuna.com, which uses this action, and a similar project, the 4th episode of "about you" in the 1st exhibition section at the same site. (These projects are included on the accompanying CD-ROM as "similarity.swf" and "aboutyou4.swf", respectively.)

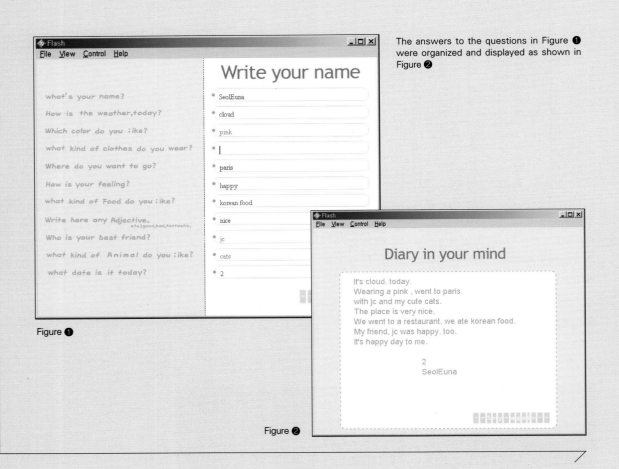

The answers to the questions in Figure ❶ were organized and displayed as shown in Figure ❷

Figure ❶

Figure ❷

After this project was released, I received many e-mails from many people. "You and I are 75% alike," "We had a similarity percentage of 52%," "I got 100%. I wonder if you and I really think alike." (100% occurs when all the answer choices are the same as mine. When I received this letter, I was so happy, that I replied right away.)

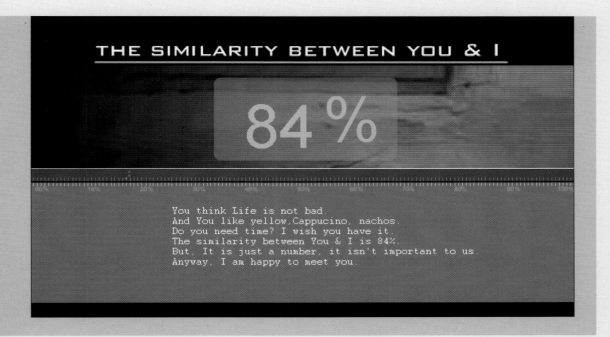

THE SIMILARITY BETWEEN YOU & I

84 %

You think Life is not bad.
And You like yellow.Cappucino, nachos.
Do you need time? I wish you have it.
The similarity between You & I is 84%.
But, It is just a number, it isn't important to us.
Anyway, I am happy to meet you.

Through this project, I was able to share my thoughts and feelings with many people. However, as stated in the project itself, these are only numbers and numbers are not important.

Anyway, it was nice meeting you....

Flash MX Motion Graphics

08. Taiyup's Flash World

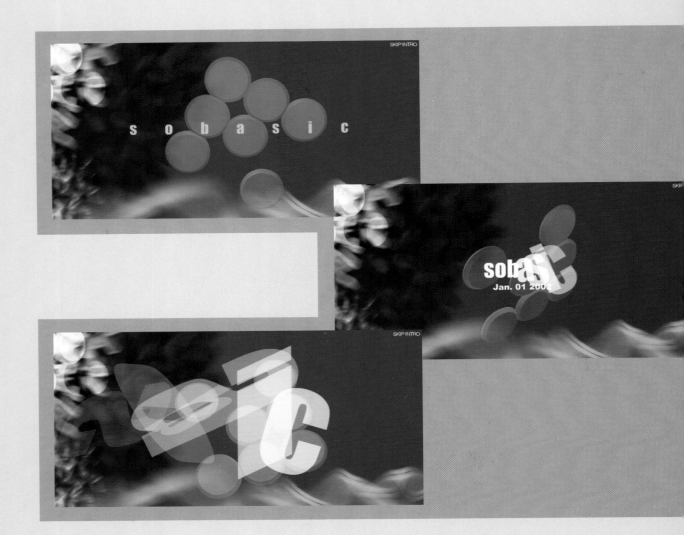

Concept

Taiyup.com is my (Taiyup Kim's) personal sketchbook. It is where I express, on the Web, things that I have seen and felt and where I portray everything that I felt to be unsatisfactory with what I did at work. There is no ultimate goal or purpose. It just contains the images that I like displayed, to users in the way that I want using the colors that I want.

In this section, we will take a brief look into movies made using text and graphics.

Beginning

First, we will look at some movie basics, such as movie properties, preloading script properties and background and sound properties.

Movie Properties

The first step in making movies in Flash is to configure the stage size, color and frame rate in the [JET Rip Properties] window.

1 A new window will automatically appear upon loading Flash. However, in order to open a new window while in the middle of working on something else, select [File]-[New]. (Ctrl + N , ⌘ + N)

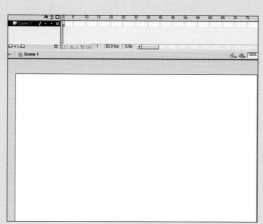

2 Open the [JET Rip Properties] window ([Modify]-[Document], Ctrl + J , ⌘ + J) and configure the basic values. We will use the default frame rate (12 frames/second) and set the movie size to 800px X 400px and the background color to a dark blue. Click [OK] button to apply these settings.

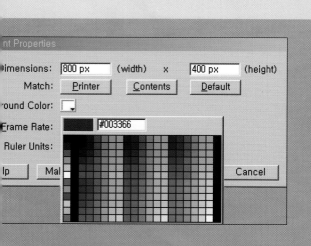

Preloading Script

Next, we will add a simple preloading script, where the movie waits to play until after the last frame has been loaded.

1 ··After inserting a layer, name the first layer "script" and the second layer "loadingIMG."

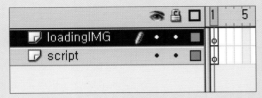

2 ··Add the following script to the first frame of the layer:

```
ifFrameLoaded ("last"){
        gotoAndPlay ("start");
}
```

The "start" and "last" labels will be assigned to the first and last sections, respectively, of the movie after the movie is complete.

3 ··Add the following script to the second frame:

```
gotoAndPlay (1);
```

This action will have the movie move between the first and second frames until the last frame is loaded and then move to the "start" label.

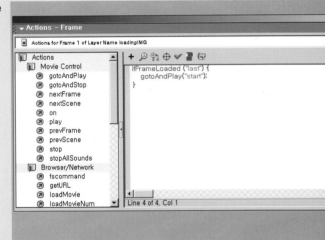

4 ··The "loadingIMG" label is used to center an image in the center of the stage that states that the image is loading.

Configuring Layers

In order to more effectively manage Flash movies, we need to divide up the movie into a movie-playing layer, an action layer and a sound layer. This makes the movie editing and modification process smoother.

1 ··Use the "Layer Add" icon to add layers.

239

2 ··Double - click on the layer name and change the name to "background."

3 ··Drag this layer with the mouse to the very bottom of the layer list.

Changing the order of the "background" layer.

Making the Background

When I make a movie, I first start out by making the background and sometimes I invest more time into this step than I do the actual animation. I first make the background, lay it out and then position the text or object animations on top of it. I made a JPG image the same size as the movie, 800×400. I saved this file in GIF format. For this format, it is important to assign a diffusion and compression rate to prevent the details of the image from being damaged. I named this background image "back.gif." (This file is included in the library of "taiyup.fla.")

1 ··Select the first frame of the "background" layer with the mouse.

2 ··Import the GIF file into Flash ([File]-[Import], Ctrl + R, ⌘ + R).

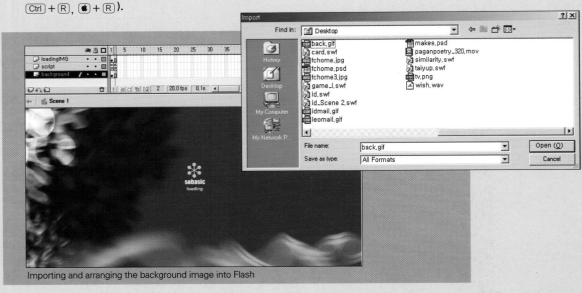

Importing and arranging the background image into Flash

3 ··We will convert this imported image into a symbol. Select the image and press the F8 key to open the [Symbol Properties] window. Enter the following symbol name in this window and press the [OK] button.

Adding Sound

1 Add a layer and name it "sound." We will add a looped sound to this layer.

2 Select [File]-[Import] and import the sound file (Jonny2185.wav) into Flash. This imported sound file is then automatically saved in the library.

3 After making a keyframe in frame 3 of the sound layer, add the sound. Selecting frame 3 with the mouse, drag the sound from the library onto the stage or select the sound from Sound Options in the Property Inspector. In order to prevent the sound from stopping during the movie, set the "Loops" value in the [Sound] panel to "5."

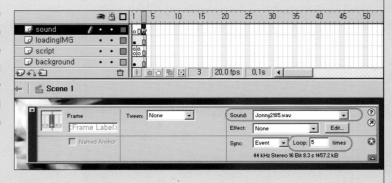

4 In order to have the image arranged in the "loadingIMG" layer to appear and disappear as the movie begins add a blank keyframe to frame 3. (F7)

Making the "sobasic" Text Animation

[**Converting Each of the Letters of "sobasic" into a Symbol and**

Arranging Them on the Layer] . . . . .

We will convert each letter of the word "sobasic" into a symbol to create a more splendid animation. When converting letters into symbols, it is better, in terms of file capacity, to symbolize each letter of the alphabet only once. For example, there are two "S"s in the word "sobasic," therefore, we only symbolize the letter "S" once. All we have to do is select it from the library when the same letter is needed again.

1 ·· Add a layer and after making a keyframe in frame 15, use the Text Tool to write "sobasic." After entering the text, go to the Character Option in the Property Inspector and set the font to "impact" and the font size to "50."

242

2 ·· Break apart the text ([Modify]-[Break Apart], Ctrl + B, ⌘ + B).

3 After selecting each letter of the word, press the F8 key to symbolize them. Name the symbol with something that is easy to remember.

4 The symbolized letters are shown here:

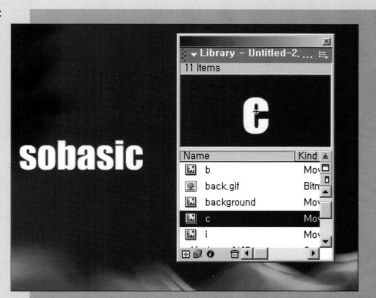

5 Now let's arrange each of these symbolized letters in each layer. Selecting all the text symbols, apply [Modify]-[Distribute to layers].

6 ••All text layers have a keyframe in frame 1. Selecting the
keyframe with the mouse, move it to frame 15.

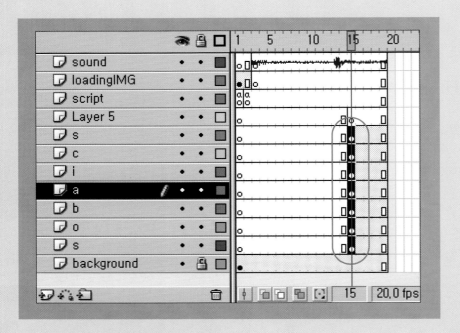

[**Adding Motion to the "sobasic" Text Animation 1**] ● ● ● ● ●

We will now add motion to each of the symbols in the layers. In order to use the motion-tweening technique of Flash to assign motion, we need a keyframe in the first and last frames. The animation we will create here is one where the text rotates 45 degrees and then zooms out.

1 ˙˙ The text symbol is currently arranged in frame 15.

2 ˙˙ Select frame 27, the one where the text symbol is arranged, in its entirety using the mouse and add a keyframe. (F6)

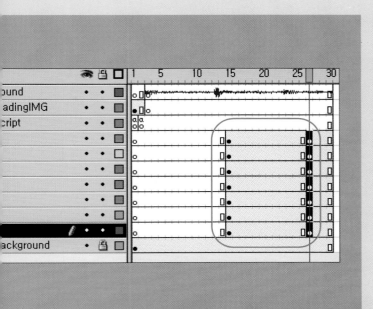

3 ˙˙ Return to frame 15 and select the "s" symbol.

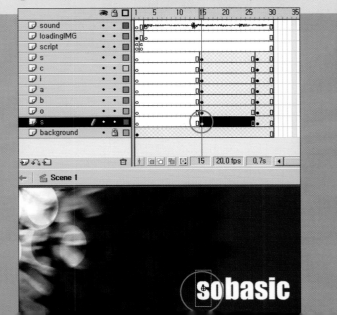

4 In the [Scale and Rotate] window ([Modify]-[Transform]-[Scale and Rotate]), set the scale to "500%" and the Rotate to "-45" and then click the [OK] button.

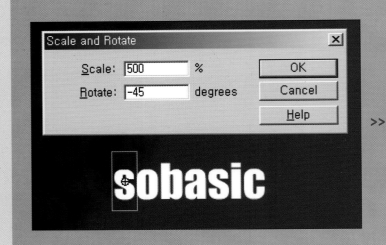 >>

5 Modify the scale and rotate for the other letters.

6 ·· After selecting all the text arranged in frame 15, set the
alpha value to "30" in the Effect panel.

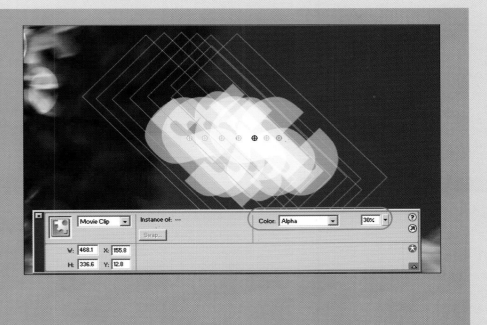

7 ·· Motion tween frames 15-27. (Ctrl + F , ⌘ + F)

8 Enter a time differential of two frames.

9 We have now completed the animation for letters that appear one at a time, rotate 45 degrees, and zoom into place.

>>

Adding Motion to the "sobasic" Text Animation 2]· · · · ·

Now, we will add a motion to the text animation that zooms out and falls into place that we made earlier, where, after a certain amount of time, the letters explode out of the screen.

1 Add a keyframe to the frames in which the text is arranged, frames 89 and 115.

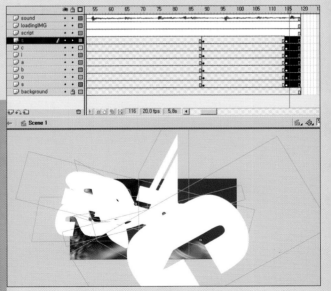

2 After arranging each of the letters in frame 115 at different proportions from 500% to 1000%, use the Rotation Tool to apply a different rotation to each. By adjusting the center adjustment point of the Rotation Tool, we can change the slant of each letter.

Changing the slant of the object by adjusting the center adjustment point of the Rotation Tool

Applying a different rotation, slant and size to each symbol

3 °° After adjusting the position of the text in frame 115, set the alpha value to "0."

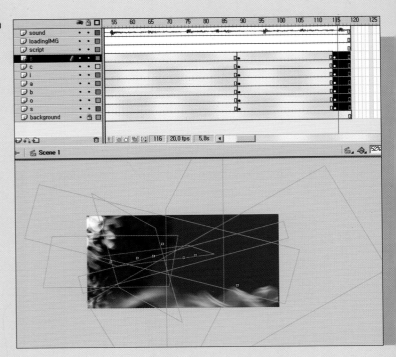

4 °° Motion tween frames 89 -115.

5 ‥Add a time differential of two frames and add a blank
keyframe to the last frame to finalize the timeline.

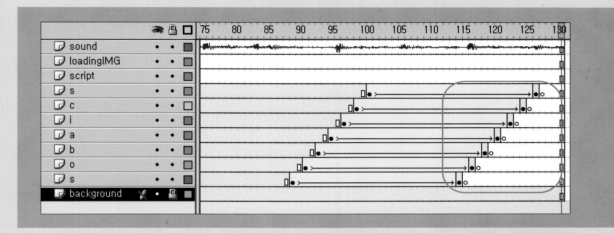

6 ‥We have now completed the animation of the text that
rotates at different angles and explodes out of the screen.

>>

Adding Motion to the "sobasic" Text Animation 3) . . . . .

1 ᐧᐧSelecting one of the frames between 40 and 88, in which the "sobasic" text is centered, select [Edit]-[Copy Frames] to duplicate.

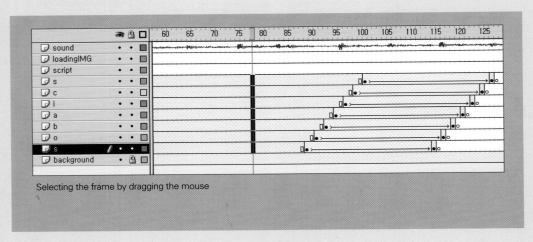

Selecting the frame by dragging the mouse

2 ᐧᐧSelect frame 194 of the "sobasic" layer and paste the copied frame.

Pasting the copied frame

3 **Add a keyframe to frame 226.**

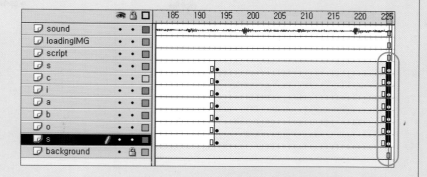

4 **Use the Scale Tool to adjust the size of the text in frame 226 to "40%."**

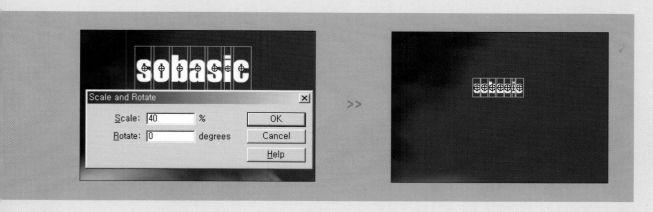

5 **After arranging the letters "s" and "c" at the very ends (right and left, respectively) of the stage, evenly space the letters in the [Align] panel.**

6 ··Apply motion tween to frames 194 - 226.

7 ··Using the same method, have the letters that were
    spread out come together again in frames 256 - 283.

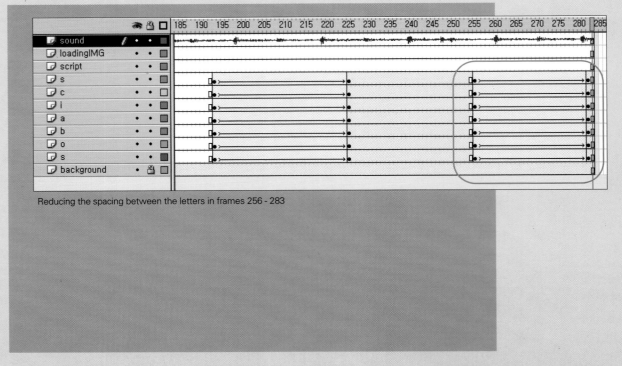

Reducing the spacing between the letters in frames 256 - 283

By creating this type of animation, the "sobasic" text animation acts to lead the
rhythm of the entire movie.

Creating the Text Animation for the "Jan. 01 2002" Text

We will now make the text animation for "Jan. 01 2002," which will play along with the "sobasic" text animation that we made earlier.

1 ·· Add a new layer "Jan, 01 2002" and add a keyframe to frame 3 (F6).

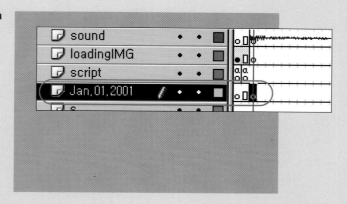

2 ·· Use the Text Tool to enter the words "Jan. 01 2002" and then make the following configurations for the [Character] option in the Property Inspector.

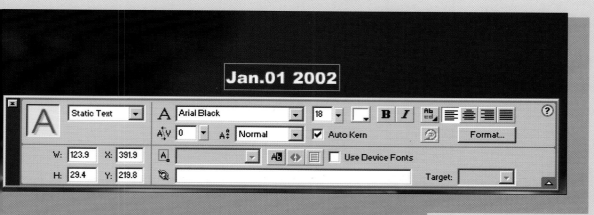

3 ·· Select the text and press the F8 key to symbolize the text.

4 Make a keyframe for frame 15.

5 Selecting the text in frame 3, increase the font size using the Free Transform Tool from the toolbox.

6 Assign an alpha value of "0" to the text in frame 3.

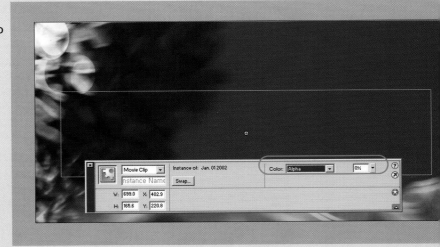

7 ** Motion tween frames 3-15.

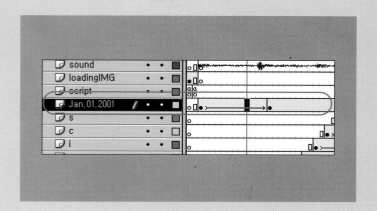

8 ** Add a keyframe to frames 50 and 89.

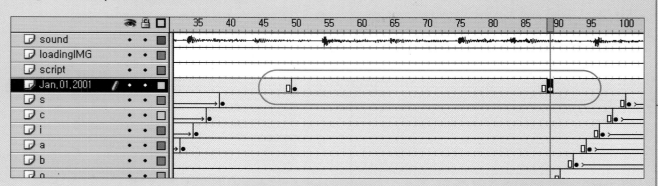

9 ** Increase the text in frame 89 to 300% horizontally and reduce it to 50% vertically.

10 ** Now use the [Modify]-[Transform]-[Flip Vertical] command to flip the text along the horizontal.

11 ** Assign an alpha value of "0."

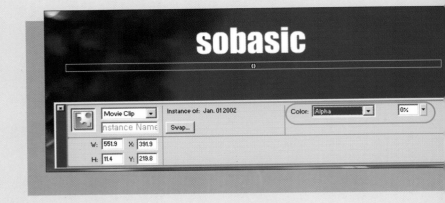

12 ** Motion tween frames 50 - 94.

Other text animation is used in this movie, but since they all use the same method, I will refrain from explaining them here. Refer to the "taiyup.fla" file on the supplementary CD-ROM for further assistance.

Making 3D Animation

It is not all that easy to create 3D in Flash. This is why many people opt to use an external 3D program. Of these other 3D programs, Swift 3D is one that offers the easiest interface and makes complex modeling possible. In addition, it utilizes the "drag and drop" method to make creating animations much easier. It is also used frequently because it is compatible with the 3D Studio Max file format (.3DS) for PCs and Macs. In this section, we will use Flash and Swift 3D together to create a simple 3D image. (A trial version of Swift 3D can be downloaded or a full version purchased at www.swift3D.com.)

1 ¨ After loading Swift 3D, select [File]-[New] and click on
"Create a new empty Swift 3D document."

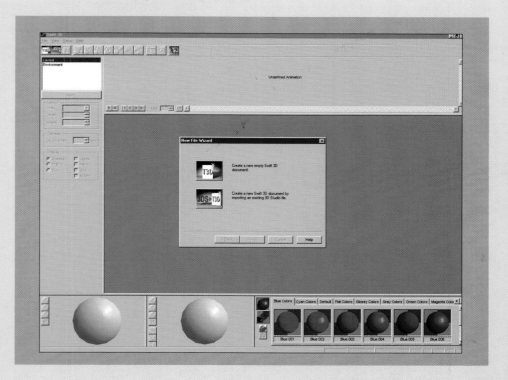

2 ¨ Click on the [Text] button in the toolbox.

3 Select "Text" in the [Property Tool] dialogue box.

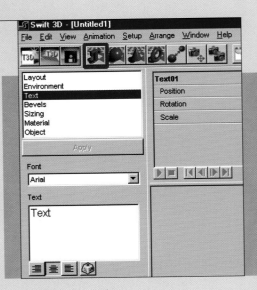

4 Select the font and the size. (Use the "Sizing" option two lines below the "Text" option.)

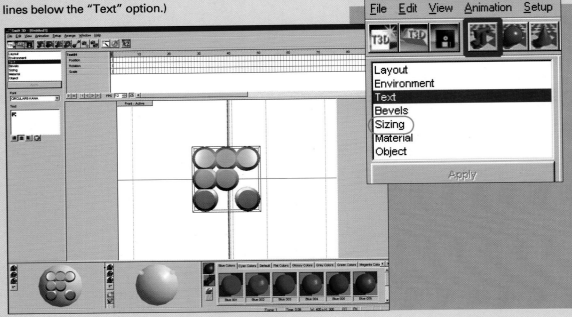

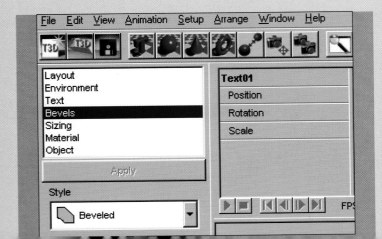

5 Change the "Depth" to "1,200."

6 Select "Bevels" in the [Property Tool] dialogue box.

7 In the "Bevels" option, set the "Depth" to "0.025" and the "Face" to "both."

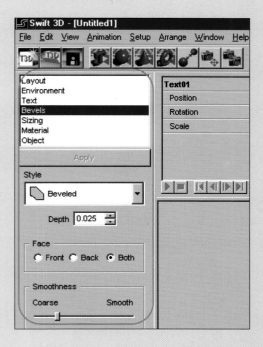

8 From the "Regular Spins" menu, at the lower right-hand side of the screen, select "Horizontal Right."

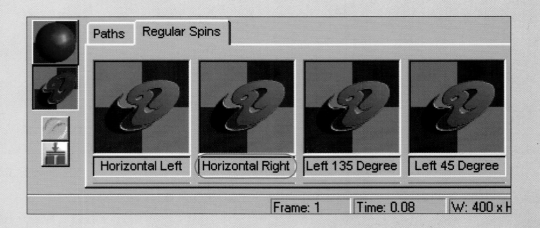

9 Drag and drop the "Horizontal Right" icon selected in the previous step onto the text on the stage. This will automatically create the animation timeline. Export this file in "swf" format.

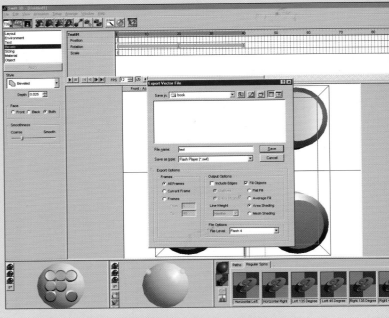

10 Import this "swf" file into Flash. After making a new symbol, select [File]-[Import].

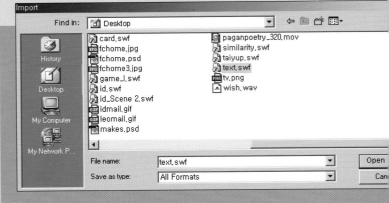

11 This symbol is automatically saved in the library. Arrange this symbol in the movie-editing mode. (This symbol was named "3D object.")

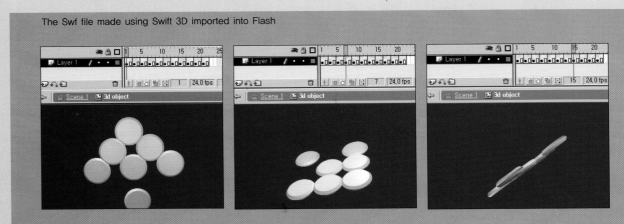

The Swf file made using Swift 3D imported into Flash

12 After converting to the movie-editing mode (Ctrl + E, ⌘ + E), add a new layer and arrange the symbol in frame 3.

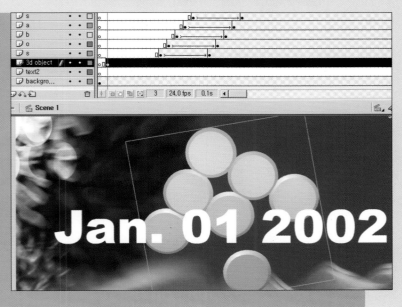

13 After using the Scale Tool to adjust the size, set the alpha value to "40." Because we cannot see the movement when it is a movie clip symbol, we select [Test Movie] to verify the movement.

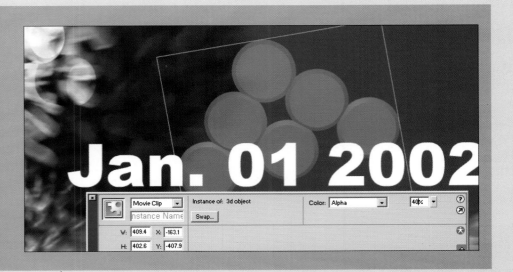

The Final Touches

Because this movie will be an intro movie, we need to assign an action that will have the movie link to the main page using the movie frame labels.

Final Touch 1 - Assigning Frame Labels . . . . .

1 Add the "start" and "last" labels, assigned as a loading action earlier, to the frame.

2 Making a keyframe for frame 3, the frame in which the movie starts, set the label for the Frame Options in the Property Inspector to "start."

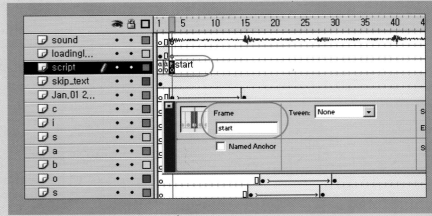

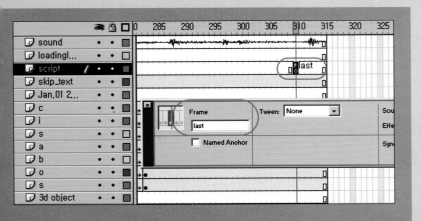

3 After making a keyframe in the last frame of the movie, frame 310, use the same method to specify the frame label as "last."

Final Touch 2 - Assigning a "Get URL" Action . . . . .

In order to move to the URL as soon as the movie ends, we need to add a "Get URL" action.

1 After selecting a keyframe in the last frame, open the [Frame Action] window. (F9)

2 Specify the following action script:

```
Stop();
getURL("main.htm");
```

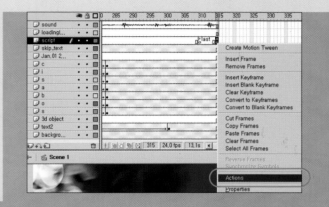

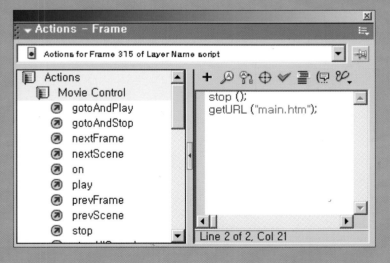

This project is a motion graphic that was made using simple text animation and 3D spinning objects. Although each of the objects seems to have their own independent movement, they are linked to create the overall flow and rhythm of the movie. This allows the movie to contain elements of uniformity as well as random change.

A fascinating movie. This remains a hard task for all of us, but, perhaps, the solution lies in a very simple, universal truth...

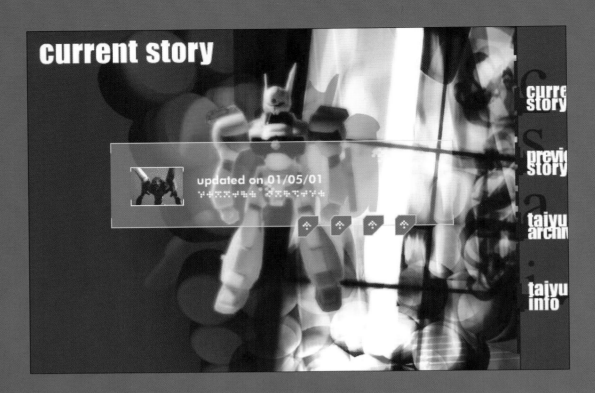

current story

curre
story

previo
story

taiyu
archiv

taiyu
info

updated on 01/05/01

new 0209
test out something new 02
test out something new
test out something 02
test out something
test out so02
test out

only one takes the winning

장난감 이야의
play like the HEROES

장난감 이야기

Taiyup Kim

www.taiyup.com, www.sobasic.tv

1. What do you think of "Motion Graphics"?

I see "Motion Graphics" as a small movie, which includes various art forms. "Motion Graphics" combines storyline, photographic elements, graphic design, animation, and sound. This combination can provide a powerful solution to any kind of communication problem.

2. Could you tell me what are some features that stand out in your own works involving "Motion Graphics"?

I use "Motion Graphics" on a limited basis in my design. I instead choose to focus more on navigation and the interactive aspect. When I do use motion, it is very subtle. I do, however, like to give a sense of reaction when a user clicks on or moves their mouse over any button on my site. I believe giving the user an experience that includes motion or sound with static images gives a stronger impression compared to those without. I also think Flash has a very powerful side to making interactive elements.

3. Please tell me about both advantages and disadvantages of "Flash Motion Graphics"?

So far Flash is an excellent tool for vector-based animation, as it gives a lot of freedom to interactive designers. Therefore, designers like myself are able to delve into motion graphics. This is undoubtedly a powerful way to convey your ideas to the user. Before Flash, it was very difficult to make even the simplest text animation. Prior, I would have to write a long code in JavaScript in order to make a very simple motion. Conversely, Flash gave designers a shortcut, making it very easy to integrate. On the other hand, Flash does not work well on video streams or sequence of images. First, it uses an enormous amount of memory, and it is extremely difficult to make fine-tuned animation like other video related programs do.

4. These days, I think another issue in the Web is "Interaction." Feel free to talk about Interaction.

So what exactly is the definition of "Interaction?" It is really hard to put into a sentence, as it can be described in various ways. The first thing that comes to mind is that interaction is a basic tool used to communicate with users. It is like action and reaction. When a user clicks on a button, the button should give something back to the user, either information or a visible notice. When I think about interaction, I see it more as a communication tool, which can give a solution to any given design matter or project. When I am working on a project, I always struggle to find the best way to convey the needs of my clients to their targeted users. It takes more than a cool design; it requires something between design and content. I believe that is where interaction comes into play. Good interaction can bring forth an exceptional user experience.

Taiyup Kim

Flash MX Motion Graphics

09. The Tracks

With a digital camcorder in one hand, I move out onto the street.

It's a warm sunny afternoon.

I move the camcorder here and there to capture the surroundings.

I keep moving until I come to the site of an apartment that is being reconstructed.

The absence of people gives the place a damp feel.

I take a moment to revel in my surroundings, lost in the mysterious beauty of the environment.

It's unfamiliar.

There is not a soul in sight.

A mysterious estrangement,

The disorganized and fascinating frames,

What could this be? This gloom...

Even in the middle of the afternoon, there is a strange chill in the air.

This movie is based on my own experience and I have tried to capture the mood and the sensory experiences of that day in this project. The strange feeling of estrangement that I felt at the abandoned reconstruction site... totally different from the warm surroundings, I felt like I was in another world. The abandoned and rusted iron scraps scattered here and there and the densely growing grass... However, even in the midst of such gloomy surroundings, I, who had just stepped off of the asphalt onto the site, was enraptured by the sensory images. Grungy colors and objects, unexplained signs and symbols.

After the first tense moments passed, I was able to relax and capture on film the strange emotions that I was not able to experience in society. The gloomy stairs leading down to the basement, an old bicycle, an abandoned TV and other scattered objects all had an unexplainable hold on me and rooted me to the site.

What awoke me from my reverie was a dead creature!!! The dead creature gave me such a shock and left me with the feeling that I was the only living organism within that space. And, acting on pure reflex, I ran out from the site without taking a single breath. The world outside was still as warm and sunny as ever, but my heart was racing.

I captured the feelings of that day in text format and included the footage that I recorded on the camcorder to start making this movie, "The Tracks." This movie is based on the small surprises that we can find in everyday life, and is an attempt to capture my responses and emotions to this particular event.

271

Using Text Animation

Many different types of text animation are used in this movie, to relay visual images. For example, in order to visualize the movement of the wind that surrounds me, the words "The disorganized and fascinating frames" come out from the bottom of the screen and rotate diagonally across the screen until they disappear. This is an effect that I created to evoke the cold and damp air that surrounded me. Also, "A mysterious estrangement" was arranged to give a biased movement to portray the movement of the air. This is another example of using text animation to relay a visual message.

272

Vertical writing animation

Text that moves, like air, to envelope the space

These visual messages, not only effectively, but, naturally, relay the message that I'm trying to get across.

Picturing Text Animation Movements

Is text alive?
Let's assume that this normally immobile entity is given life and movement through some sort of stimulation. First, strike down hard on the text. What would happen? Close your eyes and imagine what would happen to the text. Below is the picture in my imagination.

273

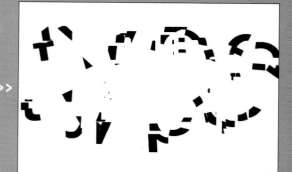

Secondly, imagine softly blowing on the text.

Whenever we make text animations, we need to think about the movements. To do that effectively, we need to think of the text as a living organism, as we did above, and imagine how it would respond to various natural stimuli. This can lead to some unexpected results. In addition, portraying movements provides a sense of recognition to the user.

Try to imagine the following movements and think about how we can portray them as animations:

1. Kicking the text
2. Grabbing the text with the fingertips
3. Letting the text flow across a gentle stream
4. Letting the text get caught up in a wild current
5. Text that defies gravity
6. Text hidden by fog
7. Exploding text
8. Flying text
9. Text climbing down a rope
10. Floating text
11. Text in love
12. Riding on a roller coaster of text
13. Text coming to earth aboard a UFO
14. Dying text
15. Yoyoing text

This project is a combination of bitmap images filmed using a camcorder, vector graphics and text animation. More specifically, the project contains the following elements:

$$
\begin{aligned}
&\;\; \text{Text Animation (Relays the overall message and the flow of the movie)}\\
&+\;\; \text{Vector Graphics (Displays the overlapping surfaces)}\\
&+\;\; \text{Bitmap Graphics (Displays the movement of the image)}\\
&\overline{\phantom{+\;\;\text{Bitmap Graphics (Displays the movement of the image)}}}\\
&=\;\; \text{"The Tracks" — A Flash movie}
\end{aligned}
$$

When making Flash movies, appropriate use of these elements is important. Think about the image that fits the project and add the appropriate text animation as you tune the overall project. Most movies are created to flow sequentially across time, from the first to last frame and this time sequence is completely up to the creator.

For this movie, bitmap and vector graphics were used to create the basic movements and the text animation was made separately as symbols and placed on top of the bitmap and vector graphics. We created the text animation separately for this project, but it really doesn't matter what order is used to create the end project. There really is no better method, as each has its own advantages and disadvantages. We simply have to use the method that is appropriate for our movie.

If the movie has an introductory section, I recommend using the first method. This is because we need to match the flow of the text animation to the rapid movie and doing this separately is quite difficult. The text animation plays a very important role in the flow and strength of the movie. Therefore, it is extremely important that the flow of the movie be observed while making the text animations.

However, for instances such as this movie, that follow a parallel format, the text animations can be made separately and then added to the movie.

The organization of the movie is as follows:

The screen divided into 3 regions with the movie playing in the central bitmap image

Text animation that crosses over the entire screen

The screen is divided into three horizontal frames. The bitmap image and the vector graphic will be placed in the center frame and the text animation will be allowed to flow throughout the entire screen. When the images are placed only in the center, it will leave empty spaces in the movie. However, this is okay because these spaces will be used effectively by the text animation. Along the same lines, we restrict the image to the center, but allow the text to flow freely throughout the entire screen.

All graphics have lead and supporting actors. In this case, the movie image is the supporting actor and the text is the main actor. This is because users' attention are first given to the entity that changes and moves the most. I prefer to use three or more motions simultaneously per scene and these motions play the part of main and supporting actors and the background. In these cases, it is important that the three motions are adjusted so as not to bump into each other.

Text Animation

In this movie, the text animation is a very important element that is used to convey the mood of the movie. I used text animation to portray the chilling gloom that surrounded me as I stood on the site of the abandoned apartment building.

I used a total of 3 text animations and each of them use the same method. In other words, the first and latter keyframes are made and then tweened. Each typo was given a time differential and arranged. There were also instances in which many keyframes were used per letter.

Let's first look at the text animation that was used in this movie. The methodology is the same. All that's left is for users to mobilize their own imagination to create new ideas.

Yoyoing Text Animation

Have you ever seen a yoyo? We snap the yoyo down and then after a moment's hesitation at the bottom, it accelerates back into our hands. We will use this principle to create the text animation here.

- Analyzing the text animation
  ❶ Copy: There is not a soul in slight.
  ❷ Movement: The characters move up and down as if attached by a string and are given the tensile force of a rubber band.
  ❸ Time differential: All types move in the same way but, despite the type and sequence, they all move at irregular time intervals.

- Progression of the text animation (each is connected through tuning)
  ❶ All text is transparently overlapped in the same place
  ❷ The text is aligned vertically
  ❸ Each letter moves irregularly up and down
  ❹ The realigned text
  ❺ Each letter moves up at its own pace and disappears

Okay, now that we have gotten a sense of what type of feel we need to add to the text through the above analysis, let's go through this one step at a time using examples. First of all, specify the movie size and background color in the Document Properties window.

Document Properties

Dimensions: 790 px (width) x 400 px (height)
Match: Printer | Contents | Default
Background Color: ▪
Frame Rate: 12 fps
Ruler Units: Pixels

Help | Make Default | OK | Cancel

There is not a soul in sight.

1 ** After making a new symbol, convert to the editing mode and use the Text Tool to enter the phrase, "There is not a soul in sight." Adjust the spacing, alignment and font at the same time. We want to insert vertical text here, so, we will rotate the text window 90 degrees.

2 ** Breaking apart the text ([Modify]-[Break Apart]), each of the letters break apart into a group of their own.

3 •• Select each character and press the ⌗F8⌗ key to convert them to symbols.

4 •• When each character is symbolized, we will generate many symbols. It is a good idea to organize all of these symbols in a library by placing a symbol at the beginning of each symbol name or using the Space Bar to adjust the spacing.

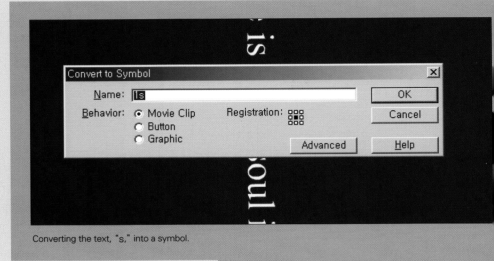

Converting the text, "s," into a symbol.

5 •• Here is what the completed symbols look like when organized in a library.

[Arrange Each Text to Each Appropriate Layer] . . . . .

Now we will disperse all of the symbolized text into each respective layer. It is a good idea to place one symbolized character per layer in order to add the simultaneous tuning effect. It is not possible to conduct several tunings per layer.

1 Selecting the symbolized text, apply [Modify]-[Distribute to Layers].

Adding as many layers as there are text

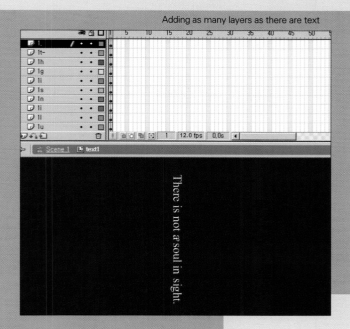

2 This will distribute each of the symbols automatically to the layers. Delete unnecessary layers at this time.

Making the Motion of the Overlapping Texts Arranging Themselves in a Row

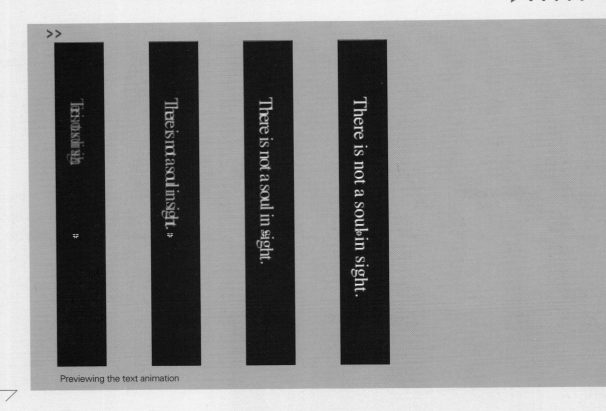

Previewing the text animation

1 In order to make movements, there needs to be a first and latter keyframe. Therefore, we make a keyframe for frame 18. Drag the mouse over frame 18 to select the frame in its entirety and then make the keyframe using the shortcut key, F6 .

2 ·· Let's now arrange objects on the first and latter frames. In the first frame, all the symbols are overlapped in the same location. Therefore, after selecting all the symbols, go the Align Panel and adjust it so that all the symbols are of the same height. Align the heights of the symbols to match the symbol "T" at the top.

3 ·· With all of the text instances selected, set the alpha value to "0."

4 ·· Apply Motion Tweening to frames 1-18, where the text instances have been arranged. To have the yoyo bounce down rapidly and then gradually slow down, we set the Easing value to "100." This completes the animation in which the text slows down towards the bottom and spreads out.

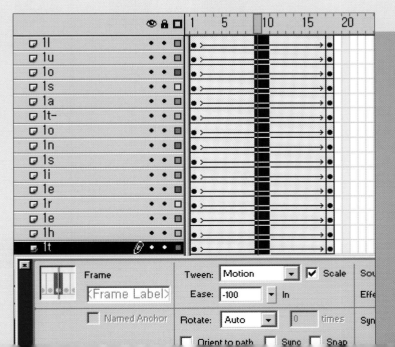

Realigning the Irregular Up and Down Movements of the Text

· · · · ·

In this animation, the text starts out aligned and then moves up and down at irregular intervals before realigning in the starting position. Each text has the same scope of movement as the other text that moves at different time intervals. This is done by first making uniform keyframes and changes and then minutely adjusting the movements of each one.

We only need two additional keyframes for this animation, one disorganized keyframe and another realigned keyframe.

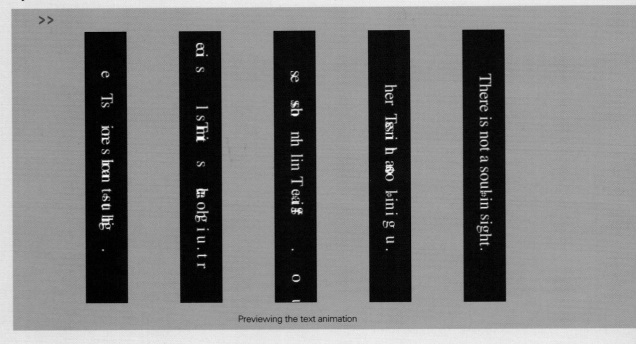

Previewing the text animation

1 ·· Make a keyframe for frames 35 and 50. The current alignment of the text is the same as the alignment of the text at frame 50. Therefore, a key frame is made in frame 50 to fix the position. In such a way, we add the two additional keyframes.

2 Arrange the text in frame 35.

3 Apply motion tweening to frames 35-50. When the
mouse is used to select a domain, we can conduct two
or more simultaneous motion tweenings.

Now, while the text that has been
arranged in freeform realigns itself, we
adjust the time differential.

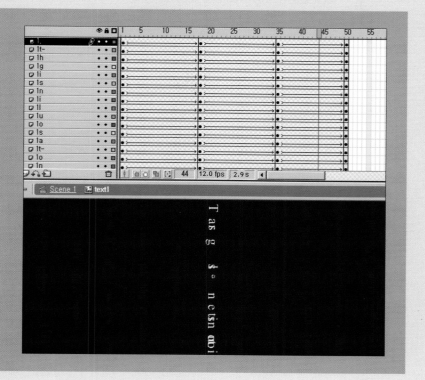

4 We now have a keyframe at frames 35 and 50, but we will randomly change the position of these keyframes. When we want to add a frame, we first use the mouse to select the timeline and then use the shortcut key F5 . To remove a frame, press Shift + F5 .

5 Play back the animation while continuing to make adjustments to the frames.

6 The arrangement of the completed frames is shown here.

[Aligned Text Moving Up at Different Time Intervals and then Disappearing] · · · · ·

In the movements that we have made up until this point, the text moves freely about the screen and then realigns itself. Now, we are going to make the text move up from this realigned state and disappear. Here, we will adjust the time interval randomly without concern for the order of the text.

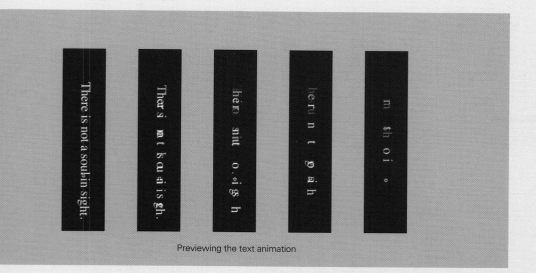

Previewing the text animation

1 °° The text is realigned in frame 50. The text will remain in this position for about 1 second before slowly beginning to move up. Therefore, we will add a keyframe in frame 60. (There is no movement between frames 50 - 60.)

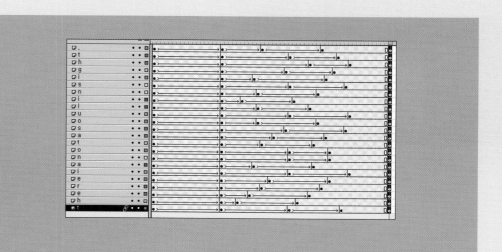

2 Make a keyframe for frame 80. The text in frame 80 will all move up and then disappear as it did in the beginning.

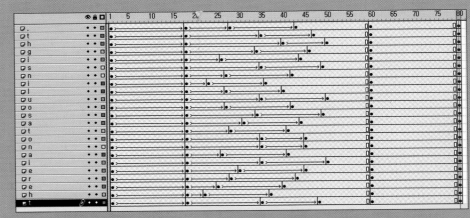

Creating a keyframe for frame 80

3 Select all the text in frame 80 and align it with respect to the symbol, "T." (Use the Align Panel.)

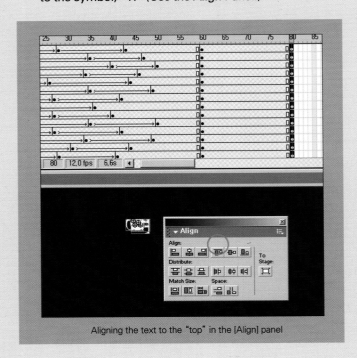

Aligning the text to the "top" in the [Align] panel

4 In order to make the text appear as if it is completely disappearing, move the text up a little bit more and then set the alpha values to "0."

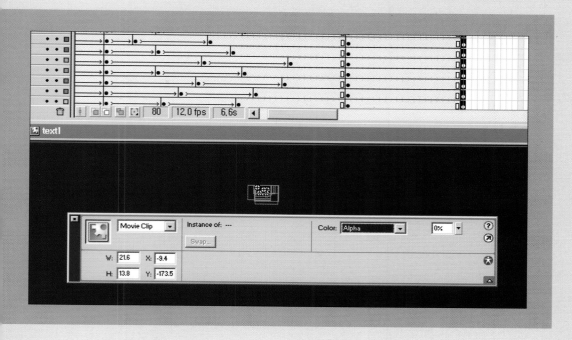

5 Apply motion tweening to frames 60-80. To make the symbols yoyo upwards faster, set the Ease value to " – 100."

6 ** Arrange the frames at irregular time intervals.

7 ** The completed frames look like this.

The text animation is now complete. The irregular and random time intervals that we made for the text animation is the unique point of the animation and is used to portray the complex and intertwining subtleties.

Letter Movements that Rotate Space

Imagine that the space around me is enveloping my body. This flow of space will be expressed as type. In terms of depth, when the letter comes at me from behind, it will appear small and when it comes at me from the front, it will look big. In addition, the type itself will be rotating in space and, therefore, will change sides as well. A pictorial representation of what I mean is shown below.

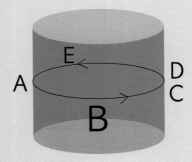

• Analyzing text animation

❶ Copy: The disorganized and fascinating frames.

❷ Movement: Space rotation that appears to be circling around a large cylinder.

❸ Time differential: All the letters have the same movements and the same time differential.

• Progression of the text animation

Following the movements of "T" text, we see the following.

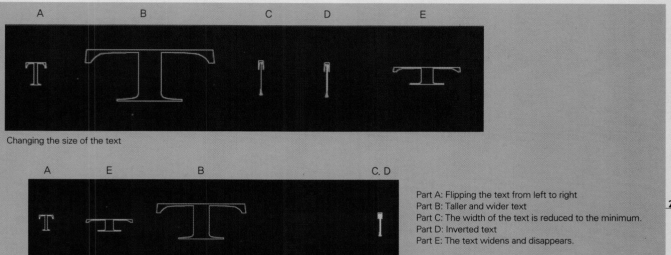

Changing the size of the text

Changing the position of the text

Part A: Flipping the text from left to right
Part B: Taller and wider text
Part C: The width of the text is reduced to the minimum.
Part D: Inverted text
Part E: The text widens and disappears.

291

Making the Text into a Symbol] . . . . .

As in the previous example, first enter the text and then turn it into a symbol. After making the symbols and organizing them in a library, we should see the following.

Arrange Each Symbol in Each Appropriate Layer

· · · · · ·

Selecting the text symbols, apply [Modify]-[distribute to layers].

Part A: Flipping the Text from Left to Right

· · · · ·

1 Select all the text.

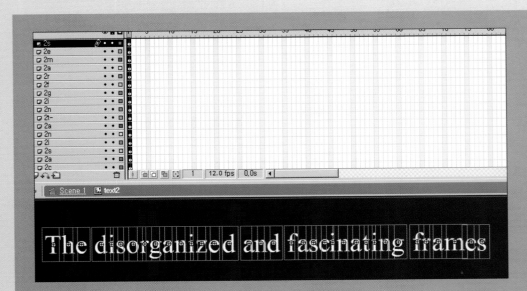

2 ˙˙ Use the Align Panel to arrange the text so that it is overlapping in the same location.

3 ˙˙ Invert the right and left sides of the text. ([Modify]-[Transform]-[Flip Horizontal])

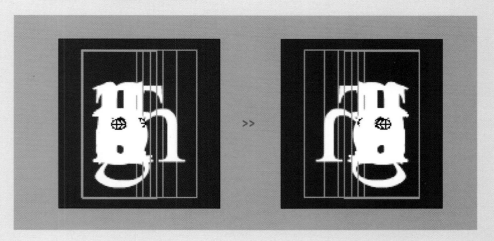

4 ˙˙ Set the alpha value to "0" in the [Property Inspector].

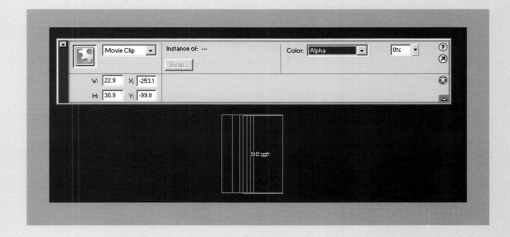

Part B: Making Taller and Wider Text • • • • •

1 Make a keyframe for frame 11 and move the text to the right.

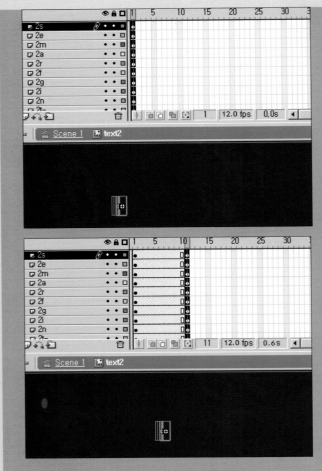

Making a keyframe for frame 11

Moving the text to the right

2 Set the alpha value to "40."

3 After selecting the text in its entirety, use the Free Transformation Tool in the toolbox to increase the size of the text. Increase the width at the same time.

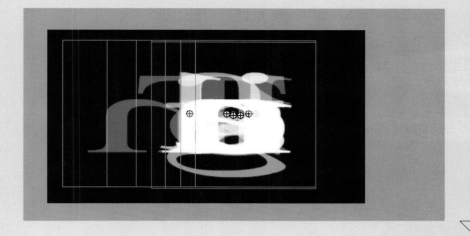

⌈ **Part C: Reducing the Width of the Text to the Minimum** ⌉ • • • • •

1 After making a keyframe for frame 21, move the text to the right.

2 Set the alpha value to "80."

3 After selecting the text in its entirety, use Free Transformation Tool in the toolbox to minimize the width.

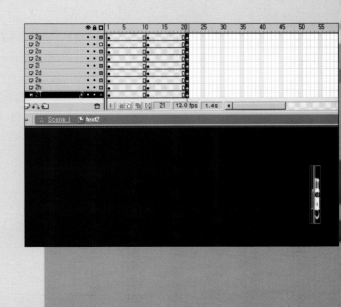

Part D: Inverted Text) . . . . .

1 Make a keyframe in frame 22, the frame immediately following frame 21.

	👁 🔒 ☐	1	5	10	15	20
a	• 🔒 ☐	•		☐•		☐••
g	• 🔒 ☐	•		☐•		☐••
r	• 🔒 ☐	•		☐•		☐••
o	• 🔒 ☐	•		☐•		☐••
s	• 🔒 ☐	•		☐•		☐••
i	• 🔒 ☐	•		☐•		☐••
d	• 🔒 ☐	•		☐•		☐••
e	• 🔒 ☐	•		☐•		☐••
h	• 🔒 ☐	•		☐•		☐••
t	✎ • • ☐	•		☐•		☐••

2 Invert the left and right sides of the text in frame 22. ([Modify]-[Transform]-[Flip Horizontal]) In this section, as the text rotates, the left and right sides will flip as they bend. Starting from the flipped position of Part A, the text will flip again to revert to the original starting position.

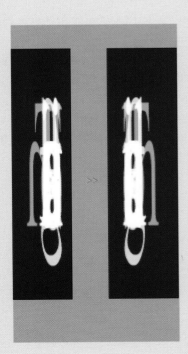

296

[**Part E: The Text Widens and Disappears**] . . . . .

1 Make a keyframe for frame 36. This keyframe is used to make the movement of the text that slowly disappears to the left. As the movements are very big, we allow plenty of time for this keyframe.

2 Select the entire text.

3 Use the Free Transformation Tool to increase the right to left proportion of the text.

4 The text will disappear from right to left. Therefore, move the text slightly more to the left than it was when it first appeared in Frame A.

5 Set the alpha value to "0."

A simple pictorial representation of the keyframes that we configured up until now, is as follows:

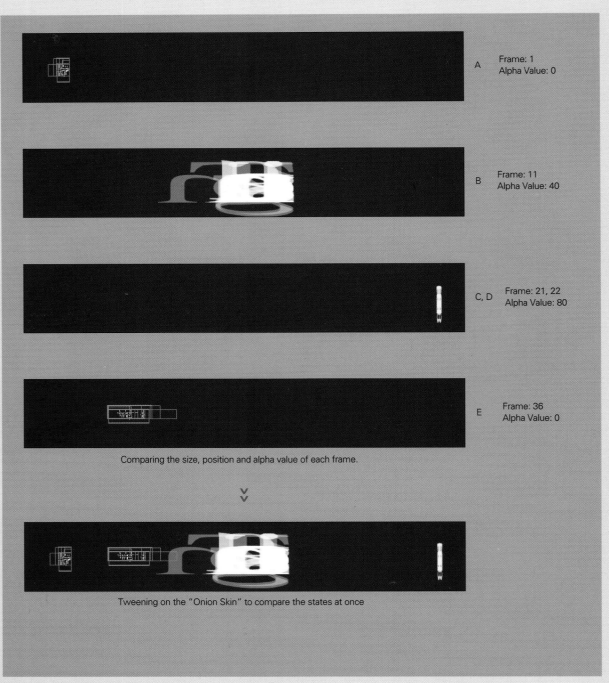

Comparing the size, position and alpha value of each frame.

Tweening on the "Onion Skin" to compare the states at once

298

We will now apply motion tweening to all the spaces between keyframes. Drag the mouse over the spaces between keyframes to select them. Select motion tweening from the Property Inspector.

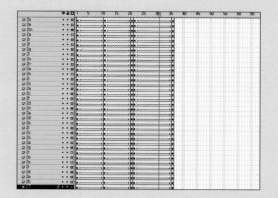

The first frame for each of the layers, except the last one, must be empty. Therefore, insert a blank keyframe into frame 1. Select the first frame in each of the layers, excluding the bottommost one, and then drag it to frame 2.

Then, add a time difference of one frame to each of the layers as shown here.

299

The spatial rotation text animation is now complete. This text animation is a representation of our imagination where the text appears to make one revolution around a large cylinder before disappearing. Just as we did here, once you picture a certain movement, insert a keyframe where the motion changes and then motion tween the space between the keyframe to create the movement.

This is good to know, for it is the same procedure used in Flash text animations.

At this point, we have looked at the text animation used in this movie.

Text animation is a very useful feature for setting the mood of the movie. Instead of simply arranging the text, think how best the text can be used to relay the message of the movie. Not only does appropriate text animation make the movie richer, it is also an important tool for directing the flow of the movie.

Editing

Now we will insert the text animation that we have just created into an actual movie and
edit it to fit the message of the movie. (Elements of the movie that have not been
explained here can be found in the "tracks.fla" file on the supplementary CD-ROM.)

1 After making a new symbol, "last-movie," convert to
symbol edit mode.

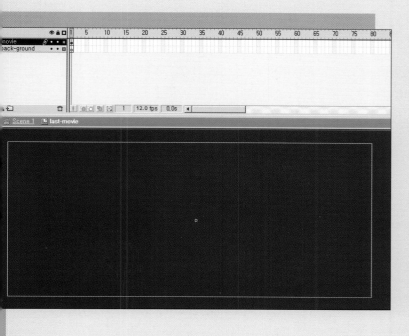

2 After adding a layer, drag the "movie"
symbol, from the "tracks.fla" file library on
the supplementary CD-ROM, and position it
on the screen. The layer below this one is
named "back-ground," but this layer will be
used to configure the domain.

301

3 We will now verify the movement
in Flash. To do so, convert the
behavior of the "movie" symbol
to "Graphic" and select "Play
Once." (Movie clips cannot be
viewed in Flash. They can only be
viewed when exported as "swf"
files.)

4 Expand the frame to frame 70 so that the "movie" symbol plays once and then add an empty keyframe to frame 71 to complete this step. Add a frame to the "back-ground" layer at this time.

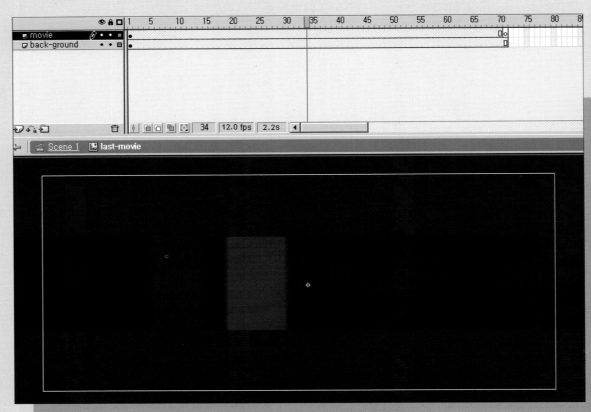

Changing the behavior option to "Graphic" and previewing the movement in Flash

5 After adding a layer, position the "movie2" symbol in frame 71. Again, change the Behavior to "Graphic."

Situating the "movie2" symbol in frame 71 after adding a layer

6 Extend the layer that contains the "movie2" symbol to frame 245 so that the movement plays once. Extend the "back-ground" layer at the same time.

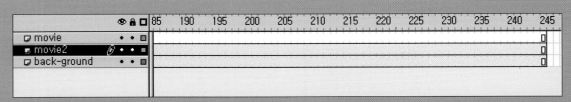

Extending the "movie" and "background" layer to frame 245

Adding Text Movement

1 After adding a layer, type in the text, "It's unfamiliar." and register it as a symbol. (This is because only symbolized objects can have alpha value motion tweening.)

2 After making a keyframe for frames 38 and 51, set the alpha value of the symbol in frame 51 to "0."

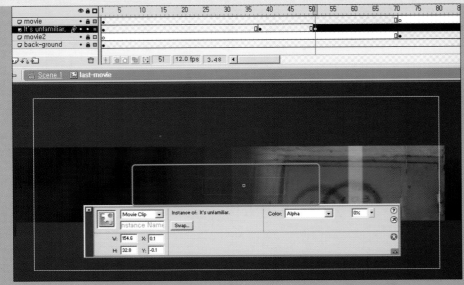

Setting the alpha value to "0" to hide the symbol

3 Apply motion tweening to frames 38 - 51. Add an empty
keyframe to frame 52 (F7) to complete this step.

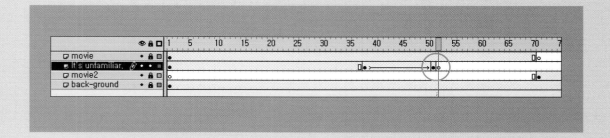

4 After adding a layer, position the "text1" symbol in frame 50.

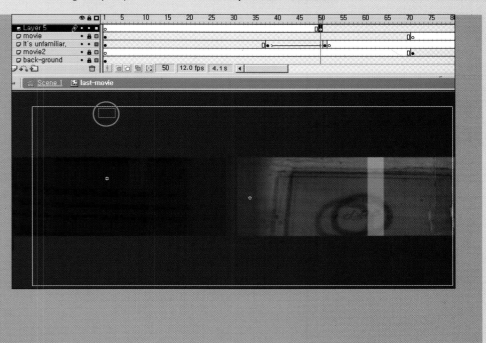

5 Verify the movement in Flash by first changing the "Behavior" option to "Graphic" and then selecting "Play Once."

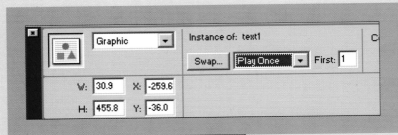

6 To have the movement play once, add an empty keyframe to where the movement ends in frame 141 (F7).

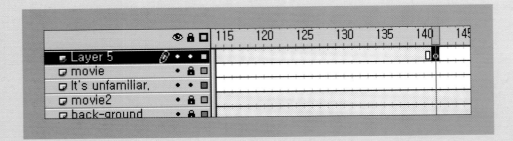

7 Add a "lines" symbol to aid the movement of the "text1" symbol. Situate the "lines" symbol above the "text1" symbol in the library. (This symbol was not explained in the book and the reader is advised to refer to the "tracks.fla" file on the supplementary CD-ROM. This is a frame-by-frame animation composed of 6 frames in which vertical lines are randomly added and flipped to the horizontal.)

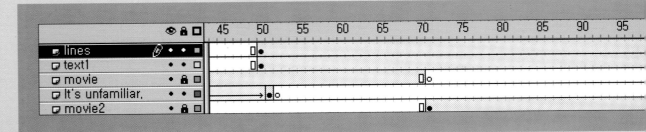

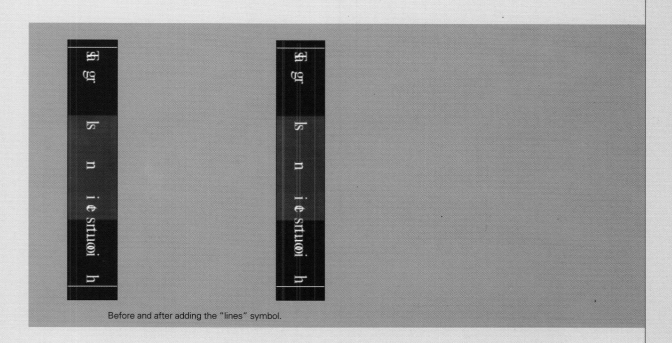

Before and after adding the "lines" symbol.

8 After adding a layer, add a keyframe to frame 55. Type in the text, "a mysterious estrangement," and symbolize it.

9 Add the movement in which this text appears slowly in the lower right-hand corner and then gradually fades away. Add an empty keyframe to frame 84 where the movement ends (F7).

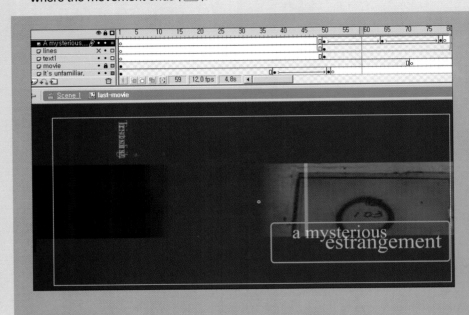

10 At this time, a layer is added with the same movement so that the movements overlap. Alter the motion tweening Ease value of the upper layer so that the two symbols slightly cross each other.

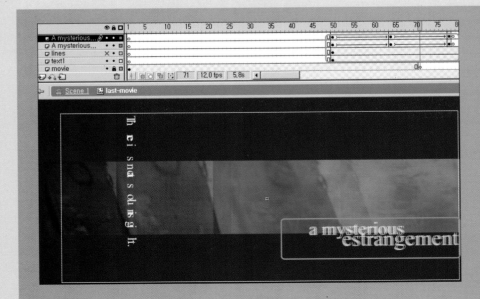

11 After adding a layer, arrange the "text2" symbol in frame 99. Then, changing the "Behavior" option to "Graphic," select "Play Once."

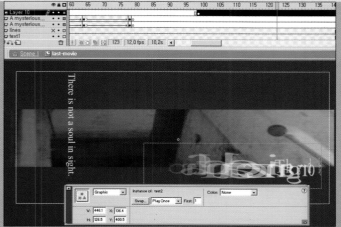

Arranging the "text2" symbol in frame 99 and then changing the "Behavior" option to "Graphic"

12 Use the Rotate Tool from the toolbox to rotate the arranged symbol.

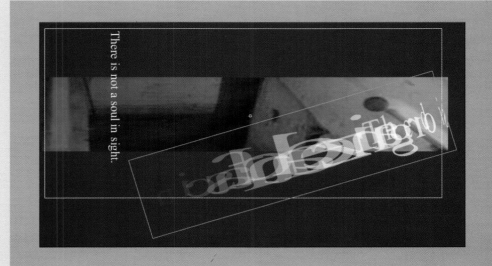

13 Enter an empty keyframe in the frame where the movement ends, frame 167.

14 After adding a layer, add the text animation "text 3" symbol, which has not been explained in this book, to frame 170 and then add an empty keyframe to frame 228, where the movement ends. (Refer to the "tracks.fla" file on the supplementary CD-ROM.)

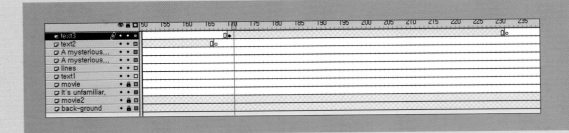

15 In order to create a natural connection to the beginning, the "It's unfamiliar" text symbol begins to appear again at the end. After situating the "It's unfamiliar" symbol again in frame 233, make a keyframe in frame 245 and motion tween frames the frames in between. At this time, the alpha value for frame 233 must be set to "0" to create the gradual reappearance of the text.

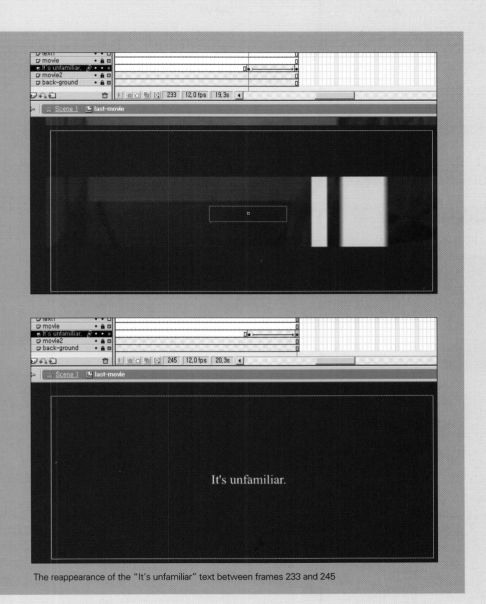

The reappearance of the "It's unfamiliar" text between frames 233 and 245

We have now completed making the "last-movie" symbol. We will now arrange this in the movie edit mode.

Making the Final Arrangements in Movie Edit Mode and Then Adding Sound

We will now arrange the "last-movie" symbol in the movie edit mode and conduct the final editing that will allow it to be exported as an "swf" file.

[**Adding Movements to Text**] . . . . .

1 ˮˮIf you are currently in symbol edit mode, move to movie edit mode. (Ctrl + E , ⌘ + E)

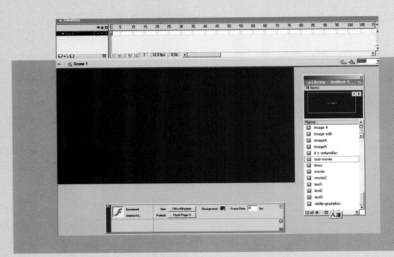

2 ˮˮBecause we will assign loading action to frames 1-3, we make a keyframe in frame 4 and situate the "last-movie" symbol.

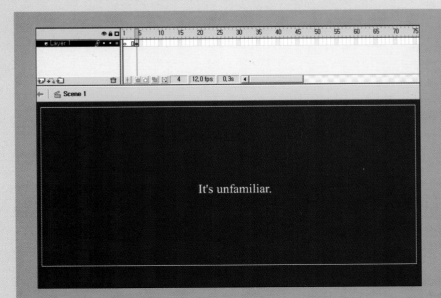

3 Changing the behavior to "Graphic," add frames up until frame 248 so that the move plays once (F5).

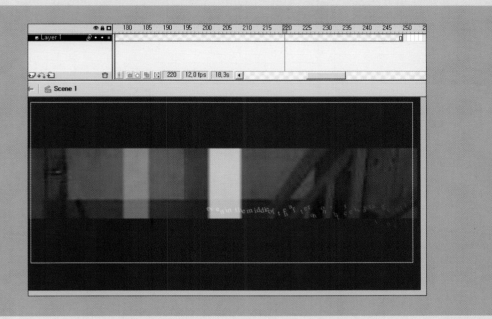

The reason we change the behavior of the "last-movie" symbol to "Graphic" is not so that the movement can be verified in Flash, but to breakup the movie loading bandwidth over all the frames. For movie clip symbols, all of the bandwidth is concentrated in the frame that contains the symbol, but converting to "Graphic" disperses the bandwidth depending on the frame. This can be better understood by comparing the two streaming graphs of the same symbol in which the behavior has been changed.

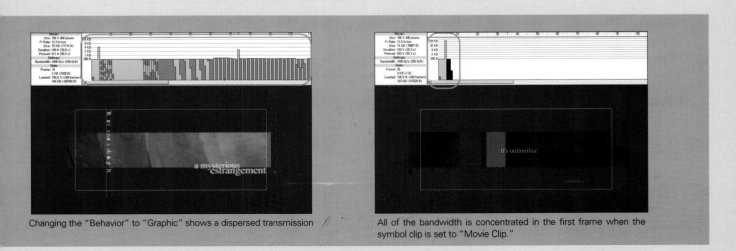

Changing the "Behavior" to "Graphic" shows a dispersed transmission

All of the bandwidth is concentrated in the first frame when the symbol clip is set to "Movie Clip."

Masks are used to organize the irregularity of the distortion.

4 After adding a layer, establish the domain in which the movie will be played.

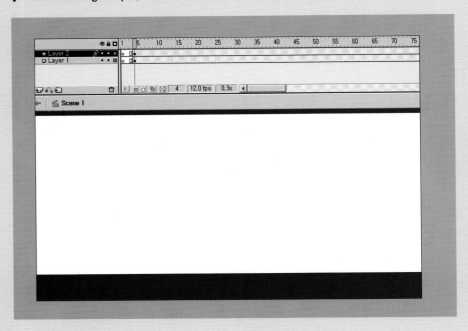

5 Apply the mask in the [Layer Properties] dialogue box that appears by double-clicking on the icon. Apply the "masked" property, in the same way, for the layer that contains the "last-movie" symbol. (For Windows users, right-clicking the mouse to apply a mask to the top layer will automatically apply a mask to the lower layers.)

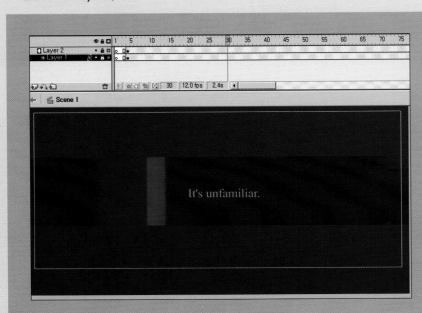

6 After adding a layer, add the words, "There were tracks indicating that a large number of people had passed," in the lower right-hand corner.

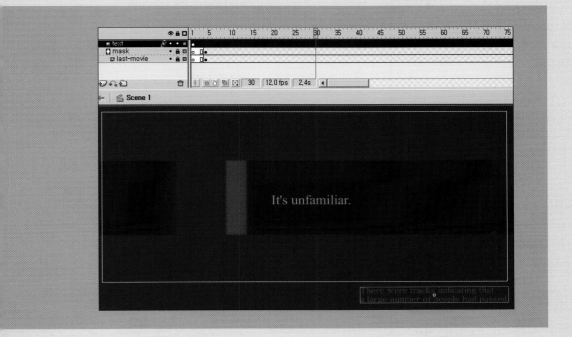

(**Adding Sound**) . . . . .

We now add the appropriate sound to further portray the mood of the movie. Here, we will learn how to control the sound so that it is not repeated when the movie is looped. For example, let's suppose we have a movie where sound was entered into frame 1. When the movie comes to an end, it will return to the first frame and play again. When this happens, the sound that was playing with the first rendition of the movie will overlap with the sound that plays again when the movie is looped back to the beginning. It requires accurate precision on our part to prevent this from happening.

What would happen if we had the sound stop at the last frame? It goes without saying that the overlapping of the sounds would be prevented. However, there would be a momentary pause as the sound stops in the last frame and before it plays again when looped back to the first frame. Therefore, this is not a good idea.

Here is what I recommend:

If there is sound in frame 4, insert an action in the last frame that tells it to go to frame 5 (go to and play(5)). When the movie is played back again, it will go to frame 5, (a frame that does not have any sound) to prevent the overlapping of the two sounds. This will also prevent any pauses in the sound. Of course, when the sound is first configured, we need to specify a sufficient loop value to prevent the stopping of the sound, no matter how long it is.

We used the method described earlier for this movie. This is the same method that is used frequently when using looped music. Let's look at it briefly here:

1 Add the label name, "start," in the frame where the loading frame ends and the movie starts. After making a keyframe, enter "start" for the "frame label" in the Property Inspector.

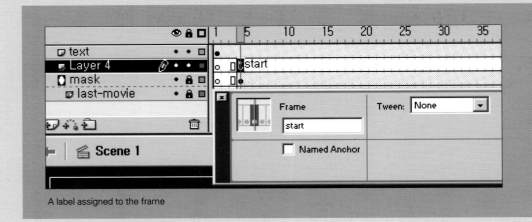

A label assigned to the frame

When a label is assigned for a frame, an action should also be appointed that prevents the label name from changing even if the location of the frame should change. This makes things much easier, for when making movies, there are times when we have to change the location of the frame. (For example, when a loading movie is inserted, all the frames are moved back a little.) Therefore, the labels should be used appropriately.

2 Enter the sound in the "start" frame. (Import the desired sound.)

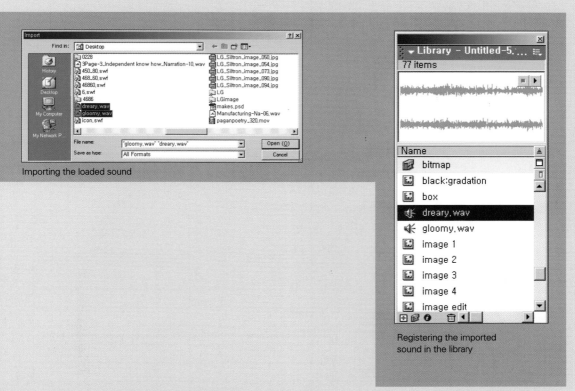

Importing the loaded sound

Registering the imported
sound in the library

3 After selecting the frame to which you wish to add the sound, select the sound file from under "sound" in the Property Inspector or drag the sound from the library onto the stage.

Selecting the sound

Inserting the selected sound in the frame labeled, "sound."

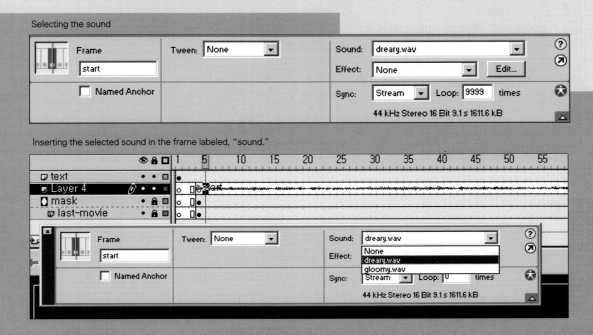

4 Set the Loop to "9999" under "Sound" in the Property Inspector. Because this will be the background music, the sound is looped to play without stopping. (Of course the sound will stop after the movie has looped 9999 times, but I really don't think anyone will watch the movie that many times.)

5 After adding a layer, assign the label name, "start2" for the frame after the one labeled "start."

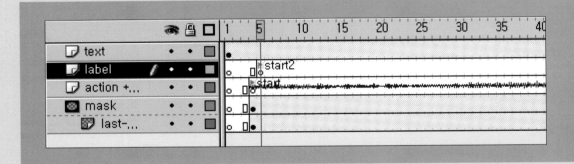

6 Add effect music to the "start2" label frame in the same way. Because this sound will only play once, set the Loops value to "1." This sound will only play once during the start of the movie.

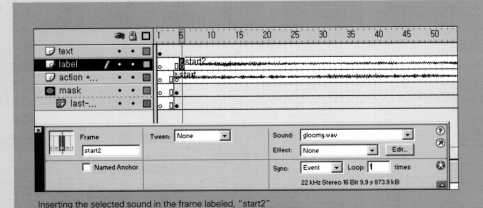

Inserting the selected sound in the frame labeled, "start2"

7 Enter the action that will cause the movie to loop back to the frame labeled "start2" after the last frame.

```
go to and play("start2") ;
```

Using this method, after the movie plays, it will go to and play where the "start2" sound effect is to have the sound effect repeat just once instead of having the entire background music repeat. This is how the background music is able to repeat along with the movie without stopping and overlapping.

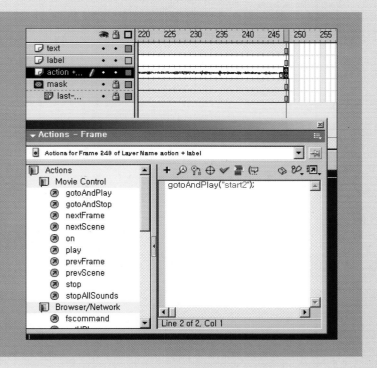

Making a Smart Loading Movie · · · · · ·

When configuring the loading, it is more efficient to have the movie load while it is being played rather than having the entire movie load and then play. For example, let's suppose that we have a 20 second, 100K movie. Then, for users using a 56K modem, 80K can be loaded in 20 seconds. Therefore, we can set the initial loading to 20 - 40K. This is, of course, assuming that the bandwidth is distributed evenly throughout the movie.

We will be creating this effective loading action here. First, let's verify how the bandwidth is distributed by viewing the streaming graph in the Test Movie mode.

1 Select [Test Movie] and view the "Streaming Graph" of the movie. (If the graph is not visible, select [View]-[Bandwidth Profiler] in Test Movie mode.)

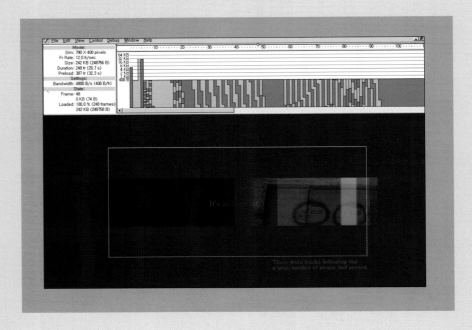

2 ·· Currently, the bandwidth is set to 400B for a transmission of 4.8K per second. To change this configuration, select another value in [Debug] or directly in [Customize].

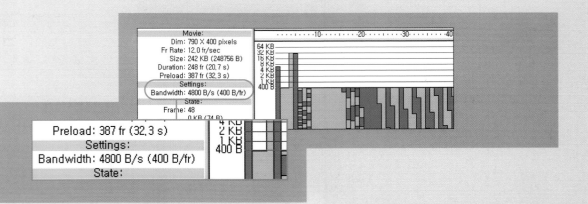

3 ·· Through the graph, we see that the bandwidth is concentrated in frames 4 and 5, where the movie begins, and does not go over into the other frames. Therefore, we can predict that preloading anywhere from 5 to 30 frames will allow the movie to play without stagnation or any other problems. In this way, the Test Movie mode is the basis by which we can decide the loading domain of the streaming graph.

4 ·· Turn off the Test Movie mode and go back to movie edit mode. After selecting frame 1, open the [Actions] window. (F9)

tip >>

Bandwidth refers to the amount of data that can be received by the Web per second. In other words, for a bandwidth of 4.8kb per second, 400 bytes can be received per frame for a movie configured to 12 frames per second. For areas that exceed this bandwidth, the movie will stop momentarily while this portion is being transmitted.

6 Enter the following action:

```
IfFrameLoaded(40){
GotoAndPlay("start");
}
```

This action means that when frame 40 is loaded, the movie will begin playing from the frame labeled "start."

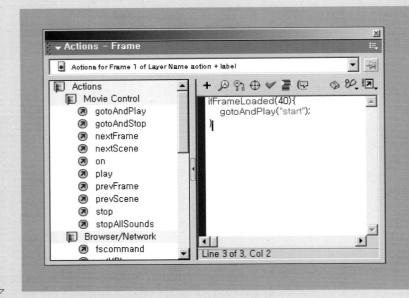

7 Enter the following action (to go to and play frame 1) into frame 3:

```
gotoAndPlay(1) ;
```

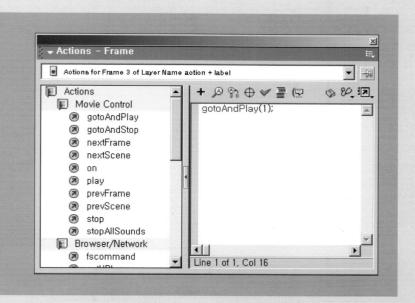

8 A short loading movie was inserted into frame 1 of the "last-movie" layer to show while the movie is loading. (Refer to the "tracks.fla" file on the supplementary CD-ROM.)

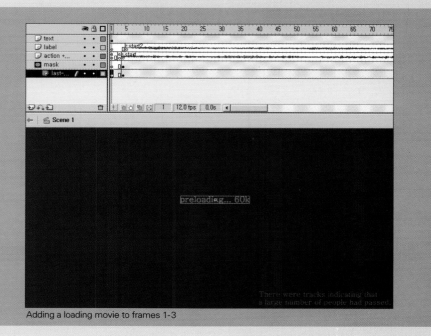

Adding a loading movie to frames 1-3

9 If, through frames 1-3 above, the movie is not loaded to frame 40, the action will be configured to continue repeating frames 1-3. Of course, if frame 40 is loaded, the movie will start playing from the frame labeled "start."

10 Execute [Test Movie] again.

11 To preview how the movie will appear on the Web, select [View]-[Show Streaming]. The green signifies the portion that has already been loaded. Until the configured frame 30 is loaded, the frame marker will continue to movie between frames 1 and 3. When the green loaded portion passes frame 30, the movie will begin playing from the frame labeled "start."

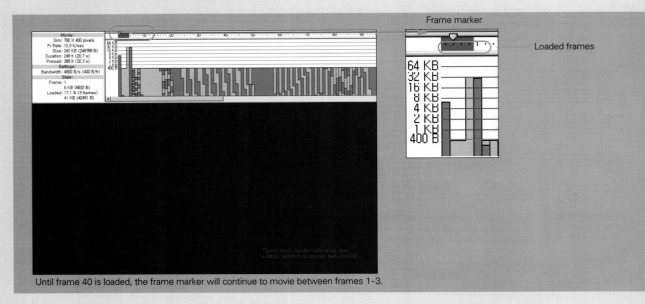

Until frame 40 is loaded, the frame marker will continue to movie between frames 1-3.

In this way, we can preview how the file will be transmitted on the Web through the "Show Streaming" (Ctrl + Enter) feature of the Test Movie mode.

At this point, we have looked at the process involved in the making of the movie, "The Tracks." I wonder how much of my experiences of that day I will be able to convey to users through this movie... It is my hope that users are at least able to feel a touch of the strange alienation that I felt that day.

Todd Purgason

1. What do you think of "Motion Graphics"?

I think motion is a very dynamic communication tool. Like sound it can cast a mood and reach into a person and draw out a certain level of emotion. Motion graphics with sound can be extremely powerful. On the web it needs to be called into play with the appropriate balance of interactivity and content unlike broadcast which is sheer message.

2. Could you tell me what are some features that stand out in your own works involving "Motion Graphics"?

Well for one thing I am very intentional about everything that I design and the motion is built out of the design concept. It is a supporting character to the play in which other characters are sound, interactivity, layout and content.

3. Please tell me about both advantages and disadvantages of the "Flash Motion Graphics"?

It is a great tool for Web. Motion graphics is basically the only viable tool for the web. We have even done some TV commercials with it. But for broadcast there are much more powerful and appropriate tools like after affects.

4. These days, I think another issue in the Web is "Interaction." Feel free to talk about Interaction.

Interactivity is the key to success for creating web content that people can participate in. The web is an active medium as opposed to broadcast which is a passive medium. The combination of motion and interactivity can create a toy-like experience or a tool-like experience with which people can engage, participate, and generally experience content.

www.juxtinteractive.com

Samuel Wan

1. What do you think of the art of "Motion Graphics"?

From what I understand, the term "Motion Graphics" came from the early film industry, when designers first created opening titles to introduce a movie. Motion graphics in films set the mood of the movie, and caught the audience's attention before the story began.

Web designers use motion graphics to introduce a website, but a website is very different from a film. When you're at the cinema, you usually expect to watch the whole movie, and there's no "Skip Intro" button at the theater! On the web, users don't pay eight dollars for a movie ticket, they aren't trapped in a theater seat between other audience members, so they don't feel obligated to sit through the entire website as they would sit through an entire film (unless it's a really bad film).
Internet users have a shorter attention span than movie audiences, and the technology is more limited due to bandwidth. They can switch to a million other URL's at their fingertips if they get bored. So the best motion graphics artists aim for very quick and intense motion graphics. They tell an interesting story within several seconds, like TV commercials. Other designers aim for a more ambient mood, with slower graphics and richer textures... these kinds of motion graphics are difficult to design because they have to engage a viewer's attention in a more subtle way. Some of my favorite motion graphics designers include the WDDG (www.wddg.com), Juxt Interactive (www.juxtinteractive.com) and Irene Chan (www.design-agency.com/project/irene/).

2. Could you tell me what are some features that stand out in your own works involving "Motion Graphics"?

An art director gave me this piece of advice: it's all about telling the story. I still try to follow that advice, but I must admit that I rarely animate on the timeline these days. Most of my recent works involve a lot of programming and mathematics to generate animation.

My last "traditional" motion graphics project was "Expression By Proxy", which was nominated at the Flash Film Festival in London (www.samuelwan.com). Expression by Proxy featured a narrative sequence about meeting an old friend on an airplane. Even though it was a linear narrative, it also contained a strong degree of interactivity. Viewers manipulated visual elements with their mouse in order to uncover the story beneath the graphics.

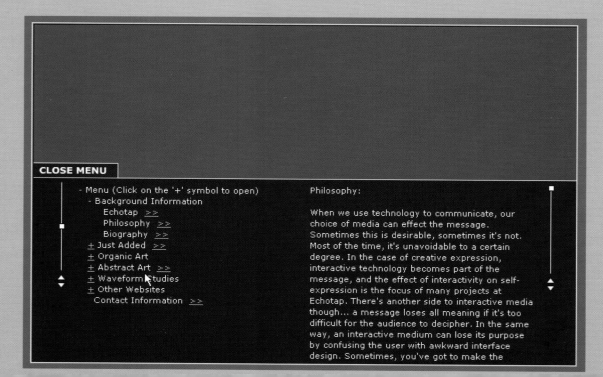

Flash technology was originally created to animate vector graphics: those bezier curves, flat colors, and gradients you see in software like Adobe Illustrator. As a result, the graphics in Flash are very crisp. Vector graphics work well for cartoons and inorganic things like mechanical objects. For example, Eric Jordan is a web designer who has taken the "urban high-tech style" to its very limits by exploiting the mechanical precision of vector graphics (www.2advanced.com).

On the other hand, it's more difficult to design something with deep emotional qualities in Flash because vector graphics are too sharp and cold. Warm textures usually require some photography or other kinds of bitmap images. It takes much more computer power to animate a photo with effects like alpha or tinting, especially when you have multiple layers of bitmaps. If you use too many images and effects, the whole animation could slow down, or take too long to download. Motion graphics with bitmaps in Flash can be an awkward process due to speed and file-size, which is why you don't see many Flash movies with rich textures and cinematic qualities.

Sometimes, you see exceptions on the web which use Flash to the fullest potential. A good example is the latest Post Visual project, "Wanee & Junah" (www.wnj.co.kr). I think PostVisual really excels at creating evocative motion graphics. They know how to mix vector animation with photography and audio in a way that emphasizes the story. I'm looking forward to seeing more of their projects in the future!

Many scientists have conducted research on the relationship between people and machines. However, Flash is one of the first technologies which allows us to investigate complex human-computer interactions on the wide scale of the web. A lot of current Flash interfaces involve making movieclips react to the user's mouse movements, but what does that accomplish? Right now, we can design all sorts of complicated interfaces with Flash, but the next step will be to create useful interfaces that give meaning to information, or interfaces that simplify tasks.

These days, I'm focused on information visualization... how we can use computer graphics to make sense out of complex data. Flash gives you the opportunity to combine mathematics and computer science with graphic design. I'm working on a Master's degree in human-computer interaction, and the research literature always reminds us about the importance of solving problems from the human perspective, not just from the technological perspective.

My experimental website www.echotap.com is where I post my research on interactivity with Flash. Right now, I'm using it to figure out how to visualize data such as XML. Most of the art-work involves some kind of reaction between the user, smart "organisms", and bits of data floating around in memory. The relationship between humans and information is a question that's always on my mind.

www.samuelwan.com

Samuel Wan

"No longer will you look at an image simply for what it is. From now on, you'll see what it can become."

Photoshop® Elements brings the power of Photoshop to anyone with a computer. **Photoshop Elements Solutions** makes the software approachable and offers instruction and professional advice on all its features.

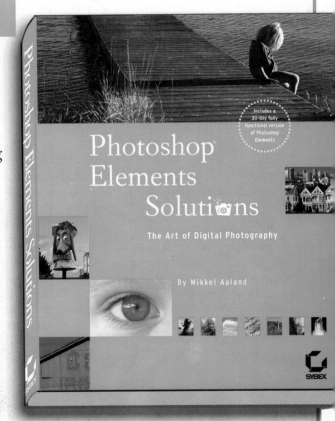

Inside, noted photographer, web producer, and author **Mikkel Aaland** shows you the ins and outs of Photoshop Elements including:

- Getting Photoshop Elements up and running
- Sharpening out-of-focus pictures
- Straightening a crooked scan
- Improving product and real estate shots
- Removing unwanted objects
- Optimizing photos for the web and e-mail
- Touching up faces
- Making realistic-looking composites

And more…

The enclosed CD comes with a 30-day fully functional version of Photoshop Elements, plus images from the book.

Photoshop Elements Solutions
By Mikkel Aaland • ISBN: 0-7821-2973-0
$39.99   full color throughout

SYBEX®

www.sybex.com

Get Savvy™

Sybex introduces Savvy,™ a new series of in-depth, premium graphics and web books. Savvy books turn beginning and intermediate level graphics professionals into experts, and give advanced users a meaningful edge in this competitive climate.

In-Depth Coverage. Each book contains compelling, professional examples and illustrations to demonstrate the use of the program in a working environment.

Proven Authors. Savvy authors have the first-hand knowledge and experience to deliver useful insights, making even the most advanced discussions accessible.

Sophisticated Package. Savvy titles have a striking interior design, enhanced by high-quality, coated paper for crisp graphic reproduction.

Flash™ MX Savvy
by Ethan Watrall
and Norbert Herber
ISBN: 0-7821-4108-0
US $50

Photoshop® 7 Savvy
by Steve Romaniello
ISBN: 0-7821-4110-2
US $50

Maya™ Savvy™
by John Kundert-Gibbs
and Peter Lee
ISBN: 0-7821-4109-9
US $60

Dreamweaver™ MX Fireworks™ MX Savvy
by Christian Crumlish
ISBN: 0-7821-4111-0
US $50

SYBEX®
www.sybex.com

Style. Substance. Sybex.